Tales from the Perpetual Opposition Culture

REBEL FAGIN

Copyright © Hyperdrive 2016

Photo credits

Cover by Therese Mughannam

Diablo handbook by jesse

Radical Ions by Eric Fried

Livermore handbook by Clause Sievet

Diablo photo by Eric Fried

Redwood Summer photo by Evan Johnson

Progressive Club banner by Aaron Miller

NCCP logo by Therese Mughannam

ISBN–0-9790390-1-0
ISBN-13 978-0-9790390-1-0

War Cry ……. Resistance

This book is dedicated to the Radical Ions, SONOMore Atomics, KPFA, Earth First!, The Peace & Justice Center of Sonoma County, The Progressive Club, A.N.S.W.E.R., and The North Coast Coalition for Palestine

Table of Contents

Prelude		ii - iii
I	Cabaret to Diablo	1
II	Radical Ions	9
III	Under the Big Top	17
IV	Diablo Revisited	27
V	The Peace & Justice Center	35
VI	Sandinista	47
VII	Redwood Summer	59
VIII	The Progressive Club	69
IX	The War of Terror	83
X	NCCP	97
Coda		108
Acknowledgments		111

Prelude

Sometimes, when I meet people for the first time they ask me if Rebel is my birth name. It is. Then they frequently ask if I try to live up to my name or if my name formed me. As I have no comparison, I can't really answer them. What my name has given me is a sense of estrangement and uniqueness.

I think I've been more formed by my sensitive, impatient, intelligent nature and the early stories I heard. Biologists say we are made up of cells, but they're wrong. Poets know we are made up of stories. It is our stories that tell who we really are.

When I was little, my father taught me two lessons that I've carried with me my whole life. Never suffer a bully, as he is really a coward, and if you see two guys beating up on one, you take the side of the one and find out what it's all about later. Always stand up for the underdog. Did I mention we're Irish?

When I was three, we went back to Missouri to visit the home town. My great-grandmother was 103 that year and everyone thought it would be cute to put me on her lap, as there were 100 years between us. Then she told me a story that I remember to this day. The year was 1955.

"See that barn, boy?" she said. "Well, when I was a

young girl, right after the war, some men came up on horses, shooting rifles and hollering. My mother came to the door. I stood behind her with my sister. One of the men told her, 'We're the James Gang.' She said: 'You are not. I know Zerelda and Robert's children and you're not them.' The man growled at my mother. I was scared! When they began burning down the barn, mother told us to go upstairs to our bedroom. Later that day, I watched from my upstairs window as those men were brought back on foot with their hands tied behind them. They were being herded along by men on horses with rifles. The men on horseback were the real James and Younger brothers and they made those men rebuild that very barn you're looking at now, boy."

By the time I heard about Robin Hood, it was a familiar story.

My mother would light a green, bay leaf scented candle and put it in the window every Christmas. As I got older, it sparked my curiosity. I asked her about it and she told me that in the old country at Christmas, Easter and other high holidays, the Czar would call for a pogrom. These were evil times, when Christians would beat up and even kill Jews, just for being Jewish. I was shocked. I told her that wasn't fair! She agreed. Then she told me that our family, along with many other Catholic families, thought so too. They would burn long, green candles in their windows as a sign to Jews that this was a safe place to hide. I've burned one ever since.

Yes, we're made up of stories and the best stories come out as songs. That's what this is. If you listen carefully you can hear the music in the telling. Many people know this song. It has many verses. These are merely my verses. Enjoy.

I

From Cabaret to Diablo

1976 was a pivotal year for me. I was searching for a deeper purpose in life than just work, fun and money when I entered the Women's Building in Cotati, California that warm Wednesday night. I was searching for community.

Inside this hundred-year-old building, people were lined up to receive fine, vegetarian meals for $2.50. There was a soda/beer/juice bar and a guy on a small stage singing and playing guitar. Once I got my plate, I joined people at a long communal table. Although we were strangers, it felt like we were family. Kids were running around, shouting. People were laughing and eating. I saw a small boy, of perhaps three, mesmerized by a guy playing the guitar and singing The Teddy Bears Picnic in a deep bass voice. The old wooden building hummed with the warmth of community.

I asked one of the servers where the money went and she told me that they used it to provide better meals for the following week. I was hooked. I uttered those words that have opened up so many doors for me. I asked her where I could help. She said they needed someone to run the bar, so I became the bartender.

These dinners were run by Vito's girls from Free Store ("You can get anything you need at the free store"). Vito was a dancer and the folks from Free Store loved to dance. Before long, Wednesday night dinners evolved into weekend dances. The large wooden floor demanded it. The community supported it and soon we had live music, five nights a week. By 1977, the Women's Building had become the Cotati Cabaret and I became the manager. In addition to this, I worked at a new and used record store, Backdoor Records, two days a week. I also wrote articles and sold ads for the Sonoma County Stump. Between the three, I made rent and lived comfortably.

At one Wednesday night supper, I met Monty. He lived in a converted UPS truck and was looking for a place to park it where the weeds were tall enough to conceal it. I offered him my place. We became friends.

During this time there was a growing awareness of the dangers of nuclear power. In California, the focus was on the oft-postponed Diablo Canyon Nuclear Power Plant. This reactor had originally been destined for the Sonoma Coast, but due to the efforts of one woman, it had been relocated to San Luis Obispo. In Santa Rosa there was a meeting of concerned citizens. We decided that we would organize volunteers in our area to participate in the Abalone Alliance's upcoming blockade at Diablo Canyon. As we were based in Sonoma County, we named our organization SONOMore Atomics.

The Cotati Cabaret put me in touch with local and national bands. It also provided a resource we could use. I arranged things so that Monty and his girlfriend, Darlene, could use the club to conduct daylong, nonviolent trainings. Monty and Darlene had been training folks on nonviolent resistance for quite some time. They'd learned it from the American Friends Service Committee. The pending blockade of Diablo Canyon was well organized. This was not the 60s with an everyman-for-himself mentality. Instead, all participants would have a common frame of reference, as the organizers insisted that all who engaged in the blockade take nonviolent training and operate as a member of an affinity group. I did my training in 1977, but left for work prior to joining an affinity group.

In 1979, several important events happened. The movie The China Syndrome was released and the power plant at Three Mile Island had its near meltdown. When the movie mentioned that radiation from a meltdown would be enough to radiate a state the size of Pennsylvania, a shiver ran down our collective spines.

We posted SONOMore Atomics flyers throughout the county, asking people to take nonviolent training and prepare to get arrested to stop the construction of the Diablo Canyon Nuclear Power Plant. Times and places for trainings were announced. Local press and radio discussed the issue. The community was waking up and moving. We spent time educating, fund raising and training people. We held special showings of the movie *No Nukes*. Barry and I decided that we would produce shows in the Cotati Park with bands and speakers as a way of doing outreach. The Cabaret afforded me contact with bands and a sound technician, so I organized the entertainment while Barry met with SONOMore and the city. From 1978 to1981, we held free shows in the park with one acoustic act, four electric ones, speakers in between and tables with information. We had to pay the city $20 to use the park and we thought that was outrageous at the time. The Harvest Band, Ashley Cleveland, Silverado, Billy Prine, Aircastle, Gitano, Bristlecone, Kokomo, De Colores and others played. The bands got $10 each for gas and a good slot at the Cabaret in the upcoming months. By today's standards, our costs were incredibly low. We even did a show out on the Russian River with Emmy Lou Harris and Collins & Levine. Over time, the issues of the Bohemian Grove Action Network and People for Peace in Central America would join our anti-nuclear focus.

We knew people would hesitate to get arrested on purpose. We needed to show them that it didn't hurt. To do this, a group of us built a couple of barrels of fake radioactive waste and placed them in a wheelbarrow. Starting at the gates of the Bohemian Grove, a birthplace of the bomb, groups of activists, including Barry and Don, worked in relays over three days to roll the wheelbarrow up to PG&E's office in Santa Rosa. Monty, Elke, myself and three others brought it inside the building. We asked PG&E what we should do with the waste. They said they didn't know. We said we'd wait until they did. We were arrested for trespassing, held for a few hours and released. All charges were dropped at arraignment. It didn't hurt and it felt very, very different from unintended arrests. Getting arrested for doing right is empowering!

The licensing for the plant was halted in 1979. This gave us time to prepare. Construction on the plant was scheduled to renew in February or March of 1981. Citizen protests had brought about this delay. Now we needed to use the time it had bought us effectively.

We started a magazine called Nuke Notes. I helped type it on a typewriter. Organizing, in these pre-computer days, meant making flyers and handing them out in shopping centers, beside freeway off ramps, at colleges, coffee houses, etc. It meant meeting with people and organizing months ahead of an action.

In 1981, the three-week blockade began. The Abalone Alliance was the umbrella group that regional clusters, like SONOMore Atomics, joined. Within these clusters, individual affinity groups designed and conducted their own actions, using the guidelines of the nonviolent code. These groups had names like the CHP (Cazadero Hill People), Grapes of Wrath, Chuckleheads, and Karen Silkwood. This decentralization provided for greater democracy and autonomy over our actions. The Abalone Alliance set up a base camp near the power plant on the costal side of San Luis Obispo.

In 1981, I was working at a smaller club/pizza place called West of the Laguna. Many of my co-workers were members of the Grapes of Wrath affinity group. To make sure that we could both participate in the blockade and keep the club open, Larry set up a work and blockade schedule. I managed to join the blockade during the last few days.

I drove on my own to the base camp. I was stopped at

the gate and told I couldn't participate in the actual blockade as I was not in an affinity group. I found five other guys and we formed an affinity group. Without recognizing the irony of it, we named our affinity group Solidarity. I never saw them after our arrests. That night, as we camped under the stars, one of them told us how he had carved a boat in the tradition of his ancestors and sailed from Hawaii to California alone in preparation for this action. He called on his ancestors to protect him. This was a depth of involvement I had not encountered before. It would not be the last.

The next day, I got up before dawn to check out the Peace Camp. There were showers, a kitchen and a planning area with maps on a wood wall for back country actions. I saw some Revolutionary Communist Party (RCP) members trying to incite violence from the blockaders. The camp peace keepers surrounded these folks and without violence, walked them off site. It was impressive. I boarded the bus for the entrance to the power plant.

It was early morning. The bright red sun was just starting to break through the fog. There was noise and confusion. Drummers, people chanting and singing. Cars lined up, their headlights a blur in the foggy dark. Cops shouting into bull horns. Cameras and news people. Affinity groups were trying to figure out what to do. Someone grabbed my arm and we marched out into the street, sat down and stopped the cars in front of us. I was tapped by a cop and arose. My arresting officer was a woman who had a Hindu tattoo on the web of her hand. I commented on it and she muttered that it was from a long time ago. It didn't matter. At one point she had been one of us.

The police bused us to Cuesta College gym. My officer led me by the arm. As we approached the door, I heard drumming, clapping and men singing. A double line of smiling faces greeted me. I grinned a big, old grin and invited my arresting officer to join us. She declined. Men had turned plastic, five gallon water jugs upside down and were using them as drums. The gym was wall to wall mattresses, with little pathways snaking between islands of mats. Men were singing: "hold on/hang tight, everything's gonna be alright." And indeed it was.

I found a mattress to call home and settled in. The room vibrated with warmth, love and the self-assuredness of eventual victory. There were lots of smiles. Still, nice or not, a jail is still a jail and we didn't know what was coming next. The rumor was a four day sentence.

That night when I returned from the port-a-potties, I found that my mattress had been placed on top of another. I was told it had been moved so that the space where it had been could be used as a stage for tonight's Tornado of Talent. These homemade talent shows were started by Wavy Gravy. They boosted morale and gave us something to look forward to. They also empowered us. The first performers sang a variation of This Land Is Your Land.

"This jail is your jail/ this jail is my jail
From that corner over there/ to that wall over there
From the concertina wire in the yard/ to the honey huts by the fence
This jail was made for you and me."

This particular night, we had a brother who made his living playing music. Somehow, a guitar had been allowed in. That night, Jackson Browne performed while I sat at his feet. Later that night, John Trudell from AIM addressed us. He spoke of the merging of environmentalists and native peoples. He talked of revolution. His speech made the guards nervous and we vowed to never let John be isolated around them.

While in jail, I heard tales of the blockade. I was told of a day when the buses drove in and no one was there to stop them. An unknown woman, a local who had come just to see what was going on, decided to take action on her own. She went out and sat in the road as a bus pulled up. The driver stopped and honked. She did not move. The driver inched forward. She stayed put. Eventually, she was covered by the bus with only her head sticking out in front of it, facing up to the driver. He was looking down at her face. The moment was still. Finally, he put the bus into reverse and drove away with the workers. The woman faded into the crowd and was never heard from again. It was like the single tank blockader at Tenamin Square.

During those days at Diablo, our supporters protested outside, keeping us in the media spotlight. Inside, there were legal updates and constant meetings about what we wanted to do. Lawyers would only act on our suggestions. We had to decide. There was much to be learned. I came as a rugged individual, yet once there, I sensed that I was missing the boat; that something much bigger was brewing, something much bigger than just me.

When I got home, I went to the bar to tell my friends what I'd been through. I was elated, transformed. They either laughed or shrugged it off. They didn't get it and I couldn't articulate the changes I'd gone through. I went home and turned the TV on to the NBC news. It had a story about Diablo Canyon, but it was all wrong. Their story showed a juggling clown and party atmosphere. I'd just come back from there and that wasn't even close to right. A commercial followed where Bob Hope "knocked out the knocks" for Mobil and I had an epiphany about the relationship between advertising and "the news". I turned my radio on to KPFA, 94.1 FM. What they reported was what I had experienced. From that point on, until I moved beyond the broadcast range, I never changed the dial.

As the blockade drew to an end, a discovery was made. Our investigators had found out that the construction plans for unit one had been switched with those of unit two partway through construction, creating a "mirror image". There were pipes leading nowhere. In addition, three more earthquake faults were discovered within six miles of the plant. The license was withdrawn until these issues were resolved. Our blockade had resulted in a holding pattern. It created a partial victory with momentum we could use, for we knew that the dragon wasn't slain, merely sleeping.

II

Radical Ions

The blockade at Diablo Canyon had convinced me that the future was about we and not me. The use of direct action had fractured the local anti-nuclear movement. Some thought direct action was not nonviolent and they could not support it. Others thought it was the route to take. Monty, Darlene, Robert, Daniel, Barry, Robin, Elke and I, along with a younger couple, Eric and Cheryl, joined with the remnants of the Grapes of Wrath to become the Radical Ions. A radical ion is supposed to be able to break free of its dominate atom. Dubious physics aside, it provided us with a powerful image we were glad to absorb.

An affinity group is five to twenty people who have a common political goal and agreed upon strategies. We operate through consensus, where a motion needs the support of all to be enacted. A person can support an idea, support it with reservations, stand aside or block the action. While reservations or people standing aside call for some fine tuning of the idea, a block is serious. It's usually done for ethical reasons. It is rarely used. The idea isn't about winning, it's about what the body collective can create. An affinity group is a collective body, greater than the parts that compose it. I think of it as the next step in human evolution.

A facilitator runs, but does not boss, the meeting. A recorder writes down what transpires. We also have a time keeper so that meetings don't drag on and a vibes watcher, who makes sure people's feelings are respected. Everyone gets a chance to be heard this way. Over time, the formality of this system became internalized and it just became the way we operated. We also started our own pattern, where some of us would come up with the initial idea for an action, others would work out the details and still others dealt with the practical logistics of the proposed action. We operated like a body, with each "organ" doing its job so that the body could thrive. Once babies started appearing, we'd rotate childcare in an unspoken manner that felt quite natural.

These affinity groups sent spokespersons to larger, cluster meetings. A cluster is a regional organization made up of affinity groups. Ours was SONOMore Atomics. Each cluster sent a representative to the state meetings. This is how the smaller group, the affinity group, retained independence within the larger body. In order to be successful, we met regularly, frequently at Larry's house in Sebastopol. His place became Ions Central. When we planned for actions, some of us would volunteer to risk arrest, go to jail, deal with court, etc. One of us would be the media spokes, who'd clarify our message to the media. Some worked with legal, while other did support. Support is as important as risking arrest. Without support, this system doesn't work. Support folks did everything from watering your plants at home to being in court when you went to trial. No action would be successful without the merging of all these elements.

A word about our strategy. It was multifaceted. Usually, we held a large legal rally and invited the media. Then some folks would break off for a mass arrest action. The media would document this. When you have lots of people in jail, each asking for an individual jury trial, it clogs up the court calendar and adds pressure to the legal system. Our lawyers negotiated with the courts, while we planned and organized within jail. We would agree to a group trial if they would meet our demands. This is a negotiated process, so we frequently had to compromise on some of our points. Solidarity can never be compromised for this strategy to succeed.

As well as direct action groups, the anti-nuclear movement also birthed research groups. One of the most thorough of these was the Bohemian Grove Action Network. This organization was founded by Mary who lived nearby the entrance to the Grove.

The Bohemian Grove is a vacation spot for the men who rule the world. It is located in western Sonoma County. While most of us would agree that it is a good idea for the rulers of the world to relax occasionally, that's not all they do there. They also make secret deals that affect us all. It was at the Grove where the Manhattan Project was first discussed. Naturally, this place is guarded. It is a boy's club, with an exclusively all male membership. Hooker trade in town always goes up during their two-week encampment.

Outside the gates to the Grove, the Bohemian Grove Action Network set up picket lines and a well-researched, information booth with facts about the members and their guests. The Bohemian Grove Action Network's greatest contribution to the movement was this research about the men who rule the world. We helped spread the word of who was there and what they were doing. War criminals were a common sight there. I once saw Henry Kissinger arrive in a yellow, Mustang convertible with a blond under each arm. Gee, what a man. We increased our presence at the gate. The Grove responded by occupying pubic streets and guarding them with sheriffs. One year a women's group laced the woods with yarn in response to the Grove's motto of weaving spiders come not here. Another year, we took to the hills with drums and as the men of the Grove began their ceremony called the Cremation of Care, we took turns drumming in the woods. The ceremony would stop. Security was called, but when they got to where they thought the drumming was coming from, the drummers were gone. Then, from a different part of the forest, the drumming would begin again.

The first action that the newly formed Radical Ions undertook was the blockade at Livermore Labs. Livermore Labs is where they make the end of the world. The Livermore Action Group had called for a blockade to convert the lab to peaceful purposes. We met and organized. Each of us chose the job we wanted while trusting others to do theirs.

The night before the blockade, we slept at a safe house in Berkeley. We met until after 2:00 a.m., slept a few hours, then rolled out around 4:30 a.m. As we drove the freeway to Livermore, we spotted cop cars on the road. We laughed at the similarities between them and us. Both cars were crammed with people sucking coffee and looking sleepy. It was like two competing sports teams heading for a game, except the stakes here were much higher.

We parked and walked up the street to the main gate. There were thousands of people gathered in the fading darkness. We were wearing shoulder-to-hip sashes saying Sonoma County and carrying a multi-person banner. The plan was that we'd be the second group to blockade the workers, but the first group froze in their tracks. I watched cars of workers zoom by us. There was a bright camera light to my right and a cop with a bull horn shouting something in front of me. People were singing behind me when I felt a tug on my left arm. I was yanked out into the street to blockade. I tripped, got wrapped up in the sash and the banner, and tumbled over to block the intersection. Cars stopped. Our blockade held for several minutes until we were arrested and put on a bus. It was from the bus that I saw Wavy Gravy, dressed as Santa Claus with a paper beard, crossing the line. The cops hesitated to bust Santa. They hesitated, but busted him anyway.

We were kept in red and white striped, circus tents on either side of the freeway, with the men housed on one side and women on the other. Behind us, loomed the Santa Rita Jail. As we, the men, were brought in, thirty-six of us were separated and taken elsewhere for no apparent reason. We needed to do something about this as a matter of solidarity. We met within our affinity groups to decide what to do. Then affinity groups' spokespersons met and chose Barry to represent the SONOMore Cluster at the general meeting.

It was a long meeting and Barry was all bummed out when it was over. I grabbed a couple of cups of Hawaiian Punch leftover from lunch and brought him along with me. We sat in the dirt, broken cement and asbestos facing the freeway. We closed our eyes and I led us on a visualization where we imagined that the Hawaiian Punch was beers and that the cars we were hearing were waves breaking on the shore and we went away for a while. You can't imprison a free mind.

As we came back, a brother asked for our Styrofoam cups. He and some others were placing them in the cyclone fence between us and the freeway so that they spelled out No Nukes. A guard came to tear it down and three hundred guys got in his way.

"Seven dollars an hour don't buy this shit," he grumbled, walking off.

Just then, a car pulled over to the side of the freeway. Out stepped three Buddhist monks. They had been traveling the world stopping every three steps to pray for nuclear disarmament, and now they were here. Someone called down in front and this former altar boy got on his knees before venerable priests with only a cyclone fence separating us. They sang to us and we sang back as softly as three hundred men could. A CHP pulled up, but advanced no closer than their car. After a while, their driver motioned for them to return to the car and we stood.

As we stood, I spotted our six and thirty guys being led across a field to us. Monty grabbed my hand and, with a whoop, we began a spiral dance that ended with a tightly wound knot of men that slowly unfolded like the watch spring of eternity and for the rest of our time there you could feel the energy emanating from the space where the center of the spiral had been.

Two days later, the judge decided to arraign us whether we wanted to or not. They had our IDs so we really had no choice. This was a lesson for next time. We were arraigned in opposite order of our arrests so I knew it would be awhile before I went to court. I went to a lecture by Daniel Ellsberg on the Atoms for Peace con job and the dangers of radiation while I waited.

The judge chose to run the arraignments nonstop. Poor guy. The Ions hit court with others around 1:00 a.m. Here's what the judge faced. First came Russ, who was about to have his first grandchild. He and the judge were about the same age and you could see that there was an understanding between them in regards to grandchildren. The judge studied the principled Quaker and offered him compassionate release. Russ refused as it wasn't offered to everyone. Reluctantly, the judge ordered him back to jail for two more weeks. Next, was a Native American man who spoke about our relationship to the earth as her children and the sacredness of all life. Then, a Buddhist spoke about the connectedness of every living entity. I felt sorry for the judge because you could see that he was a compassionate man. These testimonies were melting his resolve to be a harsh judge for the state. Following Hugh Romney, aka Wavy Gravy, came my turn. I pleaded:

"Nolo comprehendo."

The judge corrected, "You mean nolo contendere, don't you?"

Nolo contendere means that you do not contest the facts of the case but you are not admitting culpability.

"No, your honor, I mean nolo comprehendo. I can't comprehend how a compassionate, intelligent man such as yourself could be a part of a system that threatens your children and their children's children."

"You're very articulate," he replied. "Do you know what contempt of court means?"

I assured him that I did and changed my plea to nolo contendere.

After the last blockader had pleaded his or her case, the judge spoke. He sentenced all blockaders to time served and reversed decisions made earlier in the trial. Everyone got to go home.

We were the last to leave the court room and it was beyond late. Barry, Monty and I stood outside in the dark, peering about, wondering what to do. I felt tired and abandoned. Then, part of the darkness moved. It was a huge crowd of people there to welcome us home. We were greeted with cheers, hugs, food and drink. That night, I slept comfortably in my own bed, warmed by the love of the Radical Ions.

LIVERMORE WEAPONS LAB BLOCKADE/DEMONSTRATION HANDBOOK

NONVIOLENT PROTEST & CIVIL DISOBEDIENCE

JUNE 21, 1982

III

Under the Big Top

Following the blockade at Livermore, we prepared for our spring assault on Vandenberg Air Force Base. The Air Force was planning on testing an MX missile that would travel to the far ends of the Pacific. This increased the dangers of nuclear war. Under Reagan, nuclear war seemed quite likely. The Air Force had a time window for this test and would not conduct it if security was breeched. The strategy was to breech their security until the time window had closed. The Livermore Action Group spearheaded the action with affinity groups from all over participating.

I was in day two of a bout of insomnia as we pulled into the camp site. There were thirteen Ions this time. We set up our camp at the far end of a sloping pasture. Soon, there were around fifty tents, a shower, kitchen, staging area and a few hundred activists there.

After we set up our camp, a group of separatist feminists set up their camp on either side of the common trail between us and the rest of the encampment. They wouldn't let men use the path where it crossed their camp site. We were the only group impacted by their decision. This caused division and confusion amongst us. Some of us, men and women, supported their right to establish a separatist camp.

Others of us, men and women, thought that it was divisive and broke solidarity. As we argued, Monty walked away and stood on the trail between their two camps sites and sang some Holly Near songs. Women came out. They spoke with Monty. The women stated that they didn't know we were there when they set up camp late the night before. We understood this. They said that our women were welcomed to use the path but not the men. The Ion women chose solidarity with their affinity group. We all agreed to build an alternative path around their camp. This may seem trivial but the point is we could have reverted to preexisting norms, gotten hostile and stormed off cursing them or we could try something new. We chose to try communicating instead and it made all of us stronger.

That night, it began to rain, hard. The strategy sessions were held under a very large, plastic sheet that created a lean-to for around eighty people. There was no back wall and those on the outside of the circle were getting drenched. I was still sleepless. Suddenly, my head felt wet and I realized that the rain had penetrated the plastic lean-to, my poncho and my leather hat. We returned to camp with plans on arriving at the base by 7:00 a.m.

We arrived at the base early. We'd intended on going back country to delay the launch, but one look at the Air Force's security made that impossible. They had posted armed guards every ten feet or so around the perimeter. We decided to join the main action at the front gate. The media was there and our message might be broadcasted.

A Berkeley affinity group went before us carrying a mock MX missile built to scale. I was surprised at how small the missile was. They laid their missile down in the middle of the street then held a die-in on top of it. The cops moved in and worked to untangle them before they took them and their missile away. Cars began to inch forward as we moved out. We sat and linked arms. As they arrested us, Joel and Barry were separated and taken in a different direction. Barry, the more experienced blockader, shouted out and was returned to the rest of us. Joel was isolated, placed in a police car and driven away. This was his first direct action. There were no perceptible reasons for isolating these two.

We were bound with plastic handcuffs and put on a bus for the long journey from the north end of Santa Barbara County to the south end. Our support people were right behind us, honking in support. As we drove along, the cops pulled them over and detained them long enough so that they lost track of us and didn't know where we were going. A lesson for future actions.

We were escorted into a Spanish style plaza, our plastic handcuffs were clipped off and we were seated across from officers who took down our information. We had no IDs with us this time. Next to me was Robin. I was a bit worried, because this was her first action.

"Name," the cop asked her

"Wilma Flintstone," she replied.

I smiled, knowing she'd be all right. I was finally getting sleepy after days of insomnia and I was looking forward to a nice, dry, jail cell to crash in. After I gave my information, I was told to stand and proceed through an archway in the wall. I took the papers I was handed, walked through the opening and out into a parking lot. I stopped and looked around. There were no cops or other restraints. Other protesters were emerging now, equally as mystified as myself. We realized that we were stranded, without support, a hundred miles or so from base camp. It took quite a while to coordinate our return to camp, where Joel was amongst those to welcome us. The protests went on and the missile tests were halted this time. I never received a court summons. I told them my name was Tom Joad. I hope old Tom Joad didn't get into any trouble, Lord knows, he's seen enough.

Three months later, the Radical Ions returned to Livermore Labs to again help try to shut it down. We knew we weren't really going to shut it down, however we were exposing their actions through the media and sparking a discussion on nuclear disarmament. Goals are often lofty and sometimes what we achieve is different from what we planned. It is necessary to dream impossible dreams and act on them. You have to believe it before you can see it.

The blockade at Livermore was one year after the previous one and even more people showed up than before. The Ions chose to eschew the main gate and opted for blocking further back on East Avenue, where our blockade would both stop workers longer and take the cops longer to find us. The lack of media presence there would put us more at risk for police violence. This time, fourteen of us were arrested, including our best support person, Larry. Seven people did both back home and on-site support. No one figured it would become the ordeal it did.

We made a double line across East Street. None of us carried IDs and several of us carried small fingernail clippers in our watch pockets. We stopped and held a line of cars for twenty minutes or more before the cops arrived. Again, some of us willingly went with the police, while others felt a need to physically resist being moved.

We were put on a bus with other blockaders. Many of us were limber enough to work our arms out from behind us to in front of us. I guess all that yoga really did pay off. From there, we proceeded to clip each others' plastic handcuffs until the entire bus was secretly freed. When an affinity group blocked our bus on the way to lock up, everyone whooped and shot clenched fists up in the air in support, then, realizing the betrayal of our actions, swiftly brought them back down. I saw the bus driver roll his eyes in his rear view mirror as we proceed on to Santa Rita Jail.

I was processed, issued a paper bag with toothpaste, toothbrush and soap, and led to a red and white striped, circus tent. I found an army cot and flopped down for a nap. There were about fifty guys in the tent when I fell asleep.

When I awoke, the people around me were excited. The

tent was full. There was a second one going up and the blockade was continuing. Guys were still coming in. I heard the story was the same for the women in the tents across the freeway from us. Over 1,000 protesters had been arrested, most under the names of Jane or John Doe. Our prison was marked by rolls of concertina wire, bales of hay and a caulk line drawn on the tarmac. I guess they figured that people who deliberately got arrested probably weren't much of a risk for escaping. That first night, right after the lights went out, we all lay in our cots wondering what was coming next, when, in the silence, I heard someone playing *Taps* on what sounded like a comb and tissue paper kazoo. I thought the patrolling cops would jump him. He finished. The silence was pregnant, then someone said, "That was beautiful, man." We all applauded and the atmosphere got lighter as calls of "good night, John" reverberated throughout the tent.

The next morning, the sheriff came to take us to court. They needed to arraign us so that the court calendar could move on to other cases. This time we held the power to freeze the court system, for none of us carried IDs and we couldn't be arraigned without them. Judge Lewis was recommending two days in jail, a $250 fine and two years probation. Two years probation meant that an activist couldn't risk arrest in future actions for two years. This was unacceptable. The fine was classist and also unacceptable. So, when the sheriff came, we declined his offer to appear in court. We said we'd wait for a better offer.

Later that morning, the tent bottoms rolled up all around us and we saw a circle of Blue Meanies, Alameda Sheriffs, with face plates down and clubs meaningfully slapping gloved hands. An order was barked and the circle of cops began to close. A panic set in. Desperately, people exchanged clothes, brushed their hair differently, anything to change their appearance. David S. was screwed and he knew it, for he had the only green Mohawk of the group. I saw one guy meditating for peace while the man next to him broke a leg off of a cot for a weapon. We were out of control and not united. In the middle of this panic, deliberately and loudly walking through the crowd with his hands in his pockets, waltzed Monty. He was saying stuff like: "I don't see what we're so upset about? They invaded our house. We decide if they stay." People thought he was nuts. In retrospect, I realize that he was right on. The circle of cops closed in. We huddled up around a tent pole in a linked bundle of men, with arms and legs entangled. They tried to pull some men out but we would not let go. To get any one of us, they'd have to beat a hell of a lot of us. Eventually, they left.

Yes, there was a spokes meeting and strategies were developed so that the following day, when the sheriff arrived, we were ready for him. A double line of smiling, singing men greeted him with a chorus of "We love you Reginald, oh yes we do" while a man wearing a sheet-toga leapt and frolicked as he tossed paper flowers in the sheriff's path. The sheriff tried to order us to come to arraignment but he couldn't be heard over the singing. All the smiling faces made it hard to take court seriously. He gave up. Laughing he said, "Oh damn it all anyway, you guys do as you wish. I'll try it again tomorrow." Then they left. The ice had been broken. Our solidarity had trumped our fear. From that day on, he'd show up every morning and invite folks to come to arraignment and as time went on, guys had to leave. As they left, they went through a double line of men who smiled at them and sang "Stand fast, hold tight, everything's gonna be alright."

Afterwards, I heard that the women had a similar experience. When the sheriff ordered them to go to arraignment the women refused to go. The sheriff repeated the order. His only response was silence, then a woman began singing, "We are gentle angry people, and we are singing, singing for our lives…." Others joined in. The sheriff tried again and then departed. Twice a day, he would arrive to ask if anyone was willing to go to court. When women had to go, other women supported their decision with love. It's amazing what strategy sessions can achieve. Western States Legal Foundation represented us as their contribution to the Livermore Action Group. Our support people kept our presence in jail in the public's mind through picket lines, letters to the editors and by contacting members of government. They worked to keep the media focus on nuclear disarmament and trying to pressure the courts for our release. The idea was that between public pressure and our impact on the court calendar, our lawyers would have the leverage they needed to cut us the best deal possible.

Judge Lewis was followed by Judge Hyde, who was worse. His offer was a sentence of eleven days and a $250 fine plus two years of probation. We were crestfallen. When we heard Judge Lewis was stepping down from the case, we were expecting an improvement. After meeting with our affinity groups, we came to the consensus that the only thing to do was to hold tight. The siege of Livermore had begun.

For two weeks, we lived on the breezy Livermore plain with cold winds cutting through the tents at night. The guards regularly contracted both our yard and our meals. I lost around twenty pounds, while my friend Elke lost no weight at all. Our days consisted of endless meetings, crane making (make 1,000 cranes and you get your wish), teach-ins and planning for the evening's Tornado of Talent.

These nightly, homemade entertainments were phenomenal. One night, Abe, a Spanish Civil War Veteran, compared campaigns. At another, a severely physically handicapped man spoke slowly and painfully about the sheer beauty of life and how lucky we all were to be alive. By the time he was done, there wasn't a dry eye in the house. There were songs. At one Tornado of Talent, a group did a hilarious rewrite of Good Vibrations with lines like; "I'm picking up no citations, no fines and no probation." Stuff like this kept our spirits aloft.

Two weeks in the tent was an emotional roller coaster. I'd go from an incredible high to the deepest depression in minutes, depending on the news of the moment. We supported each other at times like this, for we were a unit. There was lots of work for us to do. Even though Vandenberg was still unresolved and we were in jail, we were nonetheless planning our next direct action. Ellsberg lectured. You could learn how to juggle. I remember one lecture, which I didn't attend, on Marxism and witchcraft. We were an intellectual community in touch with the Great Spirit.

At times, groups of men and women would gather by the wire fence that separated us to communicate. Sometimes, we'd do a group yell on behalf of an individual, but usually we sang back and forth for one another. Our ability to hear each other depended on the traffic and wind direction. Sometimes, we'd know they were singing and hear nothing. Then the wind would shift and their beautiful melodies would waft through the air. Love soared across the freeway through streams of song.

On the night of the full moon, three lines of men began singing and snake dancing across the tent and out into the yard. It looked like fun, so I joined in. We gathered up in a circle under the watchful eyes of the guards. There was an invocation to the Great Spirit. Songs and benedictions followed. A kiss was passed around. People spoke of the light of the spirit. I think that if we'd been beamed up by a starship just then, the guards would not have been surprised. Something was happening to us, something was happening to me, and the American vision was becoming less of a desire as an alternative vision was coming into focus.

Most of us stayed for the entire two-weeks, though some couldn't. Two days after we'd attempted to organize the general population at Santa Rita, Judge Hyde caved in and agreed to a sentence of eleven days for those who plead nolo contendere. Most of us had served more time than that. He agreed that there'd be no fines or probation. We spoke to the court and were released. Some of us plead not guilty and used the defense of necessity to justify our actions. The defense of necessity states that it was necessary to break a smaller law, like jaywalking (our eventual charge), in order to stop a greater crime, like nuclear destruction, from happening.

A six-week trial ensued with representatives standing in for all who'd plead not guilty. The media was invited and the issue of nuclear disarmament was again front and center in people's minds. We had great expert witnesses who were not allowed to testify as the judge dismissed our motives for jay walking as irrelevant. As far as the court was concerned, the only question was, did we or did we not jaywalk. The jury found us guilty. We were also sentenced to time served and released following our chance to speak to the court.

The verdict was appealed and the California Supreme Court also ruled that the threat of nuclear war was not an imminent enough threat to justify the defense of necessity. They did establish that motive could be taken into consideration during a trial. This was progress, as motive had never been considered admissible before.

The two-week sentence caused the first timers to quit. On the other hand, 800 protesters and 200 organizers went to jail and 1000 organizers emerged ready to take on the death state at the next opportunity.

IV

Diablo Revisited

Ronald Reagan was an extremely popular, extremely dumb president and many of us were terrified that he had his finger on the nuclear trigger. Reagan believed in "Movie America", a view that hard working white people had made America great. This vision had a sizeable appeal. His rhetoric towards the Soviet Union was becoming increasingly hostile. He proposed the Strategic Defense Initiative (SDI) to protect the US from incoming Soviet missiles. In keeping with his theme of "Movie America", he called it Star Wars. The idea was, that once the US launched a nuclear assault, missiles from earth would hit satellites which would activate shields that would destroy incoming Soviet missiles. Scientist doubted it could really work. Gorbachev denounced it and no one seemed to notice that this "defensive" shield was designed to follow an attack. That's hardly defensive. No wonder Gorbachev was so upset. Then in 1983, Reagan announced that the US would be placing MX Missiles in Europe facing the Soviet Union. This time America's European allies freaked! They knew that Soviet retaliation would be launched first against them. The world demanded a change and the Nuclear Freeze Movement was born with the stated intent for both sides to halt further nuclear escalation. Large marches and celebrity studded rallies were held. The media was there, for once again, nukes were news.

The licensing delays at the Diablo Canyon Nuclear Power Plant bought us time to organize, so we did. We showed the films No Nukes and the China Syndrome at local theaters in an effort to educate and recruited blockaders. We received a tremendous boost when, in 1983, Jackson Browne offered his services, for free, to the two organizations he felt were doing the most deserving work at Diablo (other than the organizers, that is). One group was from Santa Cruz and the other was SONOMore Atomics. Peter and Robert built additions to the stage at the county fairgrounds, I worked as back stage security and everyone pitched in. Jackson gave freely of himself and honored promises he'd made earlier. Our message was getting out. We were getting both blockaders and support-an-activist donors. These were people who couldn't go themselves but would help finance someone who could go. We realized that we needed to provide as many opportunities for engagement as possible. We gave several nonviolent trainings throughout the county. We also organized less threatening letter writing campaigns. I worked with Attila, booking benefits at Garbo's night club in Guernewood Park, where he worked. Affinity groups throughout the county educated and organized their neighbors. We were all very busy and well aware of the deadline we had to meet. Licensing for Diablo Canyon was slated for winter 83/84.

In Petaluma, an affinity group called the Petaluma Progressives held a parade and rally to demand the halt of the deployment of MX missiles to Europe. The event was well attended and hugely successful. Many of these people went on to present the annual Progressive Festivals. Their first one was in 1997 and they've been holding them ever since. These festivals featured speakers such as: Helen Caldicott, Stephen Zunes, Norman Solomon, Media Benjamin, Michael Parenti and Daniel Ellsberg, as well as light entertainment, usually capped with a performance from the San Francisco Mime Troop. They also featured booths from many bay area activist groups. These booths featured information, books, films and opportunities that could usually only be found at massive A.N.S.W.E.R. rallies. It is quite wonderful to have this neo-tradition here in Sonoma County.

The movie The Day After, a story about the results of a limited nuclear exchange on communities in Kansas, was shown on TV. It arrived with cautions and debriefings followed. The Day After made it clear that no one wins a nuclear war. Carl Sagan's pamphlet The Nuclear Winter made the rounds. This scientific study illustrated how one hundred nuclear bombs could, in just a few days, cover the entire planet with a radioactive shroud that would destroy all life on this planet.

By 1985, the US had 11,188 strategic warheads while the USSR had 9,907. Nuclear weapons have changed tremendously since 1945. They are now all two-stage weapons. The first stage detonates a Hiroshima level explosion that builds up in mass, giving off large enough amounts of pressure, heat and radiation to cause the hydrogen nuclei in the second stage to fuse. This runaway nuclear reaction explodes with a two megatons force. Two megatons means two million tons of TNT. This is equal to all the bombs dropped in World War II.

The blasts at Hiroshima and Nagasaki left some curious relics. In some places, the heat blast had been so sudden and so intense that people had been vaporized where they stood, leaving only their shadows behind. The question became: do we stop nuclear war in our lifetime or do we all become shadows on a wall? With that in mind, the Shadow Project was born. We printed flyers posing this question, along with appropriate graphics and contact information. We wrote press releases about our action and then, in the dark of the night, activists throughout the county drew shadows of each other in chalk on sidewalks, streets and walls. These shadows showed people engaged in everyday activities so that viewers could easily relate to them. We put flyers nearby the shadows wherever we could.

The next day, our media onslaught hit. People left their homes and couldn't help but see the shadows. Some feared them. Some laughed at them. Some tried to ignore them.

Some got it and joined us. It was what people talked about for over a week and it furthered our cause, not just by furthering our message, but by getting folks involved in a low-risk action so that it would be easier for them to join higher-risk actions in the future.

There was this march in San Francisco along Market Street, where a portion of the protesters turned down a skinny side street, off the approved parade route. This street was a canyon of steel, glass and concrete with the PG&E building on one side and Wells Fargo, financers of Diablo Canyon, on the other. An overhead span connected these two leviathans many feet above us. We marched down this smaller street to the far end, where a wall of cops on horseback awaited us. We turned back and faced cops with truncheons out at the other end. We were trapped and fearful that the cops would move in to beat us. People gathered. Some grew angry. Most were scared. All were confused, when suddenly, this Revolutionary Communist Party (RCP) woman lifted her megaphone to the speakers of a boom box being held by a queen with a slipping wig. The tune was Lennon's Give Peace a Chance. They played it again. The crowd grew quiet. The guy rewound the tape and played it again. A woman in the crowd began singing ..... "all we are saying..." We all began softly, gently singing Give Peace a Chance as we walked to the end of the street, through the wall of cops and back out to Market Street unmolested.

The Freeze was growing in momentum and hopes were riding high on the Reagan/Gorbachev Disarmament Conference being held in Reykjavik, Iceland. The conference failed. Years later, we would learn that Premiere Gorbachev had offered unilateral nuclear disarmament, if only Reagan would abandon Star Wars. Reagan refused. It's not clear that he fully understood the enormity of what he was refusing. The Freeze educated thousands but failed to produce any change in policy.

In February 1984, the blockade at Diablo began. The Ions had decided to go overland and challenge Diablo's security by seeing how close we could get to the plant. Knowing this, I wore dark jeans and a black tee shirt, only to be handed a small, red backpack to carry. For this action we were joined by an anarchist group from Berkeley and a local church group. Our guide instructed us on how to avoid being seen. He told us that faces looking up at the helicopters, especially white people's faces, gleamed when seen from above. He said it was necessary to look down and have our hair or hats hide us when the helicopter was overhead. He led us up a slope. We were just under the trees, when we heard the first helicopter. Following instructions, we got down under cover and held still. At that moment, I felt akin to a resistance fighter in the hills of El Salvador. The helicopter passed. We'd not been spotted. The guide signaled all clear and we moved out.

    We crested the ridge and looked below at the Diablo Canyon Nuclear Power Plant, along the shore. Elke called it, "the concrete bra holding back Mother Earth's tits". We sat on the hillside and ate lunch. We discussed what to do for well over an hour until finally, a worker at the plant looked up and spotted us. It was comical to see him jump up and run into the building. Now we knew we had to move.

    As we began down the hill, a helicopter approached. I turned to look at it and in that moment, our guide vanished into the tall grass. He needed to get away so he could lead other groups. We came down the hill and hit a dirt road. Many people wanted to follow the road to the gate and surrender there. Others of us wanted to see how close we could get to the actual plant itself. I was one of them.

    I approached the plant from an arroyo. After passing a federally registered Native American site, I came to the outer fence. There was a hole in the fence. I slipped in and found myself on a concrete dog run between two fences. A guy approached and asked me what I was doing. In a panic, I told him I was on a self-appointed tour. He seemed satisfied and walked off. I was searching for a way out of the dog run and through the inner fence, when the guy came back with security. I was escorted back the way I'd come where another guard was waiting for me. I had no alternative. I came through the tear in the fence, was placed under arrest and taken to a nearby staging area where the rest of our crew was being held. We were separated by gender and taken to San Luis Obispo Jail.

I was put in a two-man cell with thirteen other guys. There were two bunks and not even enough room for all of us to lie on the floor at the same time. We'd have to sleep in shifts. I eyed the toilet and shuddered.

The head jailer came by to inspect the situation. He said that it was unacceptable and had us taken to the weekenders' barracks. This was cush. We had a cabin with two rows of bunk beds and a fenced yard with a horseshoe pit. The guard's room had a radio and he'd usually turn it to the college station, if we asked him. There was even a small library filled with collections of Readers Digests. We knew we were in for four days, so we relaxed.

We held a couple of Tornadoes of Talent. Monty sang his Winnebago Song, Robert the Gang of Four Billion and I recited Earth Fighters while Allen beamed. One of the Berkeley anarchists performed a stylized, Indonesian dance, one that was usually performed with shadow puppets. During one of these talent shows, we sang the Ions' version of a popular, semi-sacred, movement tune that we'd spiced up a bit. Our version went: "Circle round for pizza/ Circle round for beer/ Circle round for sex and drugs*/ When we get out of here." The church people initially looked aghast, then smiled shyly and asked us to do it again, so they could learn the words. We were all learning not to take ourselves too seriously in a very serious situation. I watched a two-day Risk game where, according to the players, the anarchists (black) and communists (red) were typically fighting over Berkeley, while the Gays (pink) were taking over the world. The whole atmosphere was light and it was contagious. The guards did not feel threatened by us and two of them even joined in on our final horseshoe game. Nobody seemed to care much for PG&E's pushy ways or the Diablo Project.

*Drugs meant pot

On the morning of the fourth day, we boarded a bus for court. Our support people were there with our IDs so that we could be arraigned. The proceedings went without incident and everyone who wanted to speak was allowed to. We were sentenced to time served and released.

The blockade lasted ten days. In the end, despite irreparable design flaws, weak security, insufficient evacuation plans and known earthquake faults, Diablo was licensed to operate. PG&E had won, though Diablo Canyon turned out to be the last nuclear power plant ever ordered in the United States.

In 1986 the Ions joined with Nuclear Free Sacramento in their efforts to shut down the Rancho Seco Nuclear Power Plant. The Rancho Seco plant is located in downtown Sacramento. There is a park with a wadding pond within the shadows of the cooling towers. As I watched kids playing in the pond, I couldn't help but wonder about the nature of the water.

The Rancho Seco Nuclear Power Plant is unusual, for it belongs to the Sacramento Municipal Utilities District (SMUD) rate payers. Nuclear Free Sacramento launched an intensive door-to-door campaign to educate people about the dangers they faced. An initiative was drafted and in1989, SMUD rate payers voted to shut down the Rancho Seco Nuclear Power Plant.

By the turn of the century, there were only two commercial nuclear power plants operating in California.

The San Onofre Nuclear Power Plant is located on the coast between Los Angeles and San Diego. 8.4 million people live in its impact zone. On January 31, 2012, the Unit Three Reactor began an unplanned shut down, following the detection of leaks in one of the reactor's steam generator tubes. Co-owners, San Diego Gas & Electric and Southern California Edison, said they'd take care of it. They shut it down for a year while inspections were held. They were unable to stop the leaks and a year later, they decided to close it down permanently.

Diablo Canyon is the only commercial nuclear power plant operating in California. It is the last of a dying breed. We lost the battle and won the war.

PEACE & JUSTICE CENTER
SONOMA COUNTY

V

The Peace & Justice Center

We got a Peace and Justice Center. Not everyone does. We're very fortunate and we know it. The Peace & Justice Center is the home of political activism in Sonoma County. We use it for meetings, organizing, preparing props for demonstrations and collating our newsletter. It is open in the afternoon, five days a week, and can be booked by organizations during off hours. The Peace & Justice Center provides a way for people to learn about political movements and how to get involved with them. It is a hub of activism. The Peace & Justice Center was not a gift from above. We didn't read about it in a book. It was not a preformed idea from some expert. It was what we developed over time as need drove us.

I suppose it began on February 29, 1980. There was an event at Sonoma State University where Father Daniel Berrigan, U. Utah Phillips and Kate Wolf spoke and sang and called on local citizens to mobilize for peace. Len and Adrienne Swenson, David Thatcher, George Romandy, Lucy Forest, Peter Fisk and others took up this challenge and began the Peace Network and the Peace Network Newsletter.

The Peace Network was initially housed at the Unitarian Universalist Fellowship. Many members of the Peace Network were also members of the Unitarian Fellowship. Several others were Quakers. They chose to meet to discuss issues of global peace and nuclear disarmament. This was a small group of visionaries with minimal support. At one meeting, only two members showed up. After a while, they decided that maybe this was an idea whose time had not yet come and were shutting off the lights when a car pulled up. Two new members arrived, eager to lend support on achieving peace. Their energy and timely intervention saved the fledgling Peace Network at a critical moment.

During the late spring of 1983, a dozen of us representing SONOMore Atomics, People for Peace in Central America and Women Action for Nuclear Destruction went to San Francisco for a relaxing lunch. We'd been organizing full steam for five years or more. We wanted a chance to go to the City, just for the fun of it, with no political agenda. We came down in two cars, complete with picnic baskets and blankets.

We settled in at a park on a hill and opened up our picnic baskets. As we ate, we compared our struggles. The people at this picnic were the people who did the daily work for our various organizations. We were all renting office space, putting out newsletters and organizing public demonstrations. All of this work was demanding and many of us worried that we'd lose the stamina necessary for long-term struggle. We needed to simplify. We decided it would be best to unite into one overall organization where our various groups could operate with lower costs and fewer redundancies. One office. One newsletter. We felt strong. We had solved an important issue with very satisfying results.

As we left the park, a curious thing happened. A woman yelled, "Stop, my purse," as a guy ran across the far end of the park with a purse in his hand. It seemed that half the winos in the park jumped up, flashed badges and gave chase. I haven't taken a wino at face value since then.

In 1984, Shirley McGovern of the Peace Network spearheaded the move to consolidate expenses and, more importantly, consolidate skilled activists, by renting office space on Pacific Ave., near both Santa Rosa Junior College and Santa Rosa High School. The Peace Network would invite various like-minded organizations to operate there. Amongst those invited were: SONOMore Atomics, Physicians for Social Responsibility, the Bohemian Grove Action Network, Gray Panthers and People for Peace in Central America. The building was really two buildings joined together with a brief, funky hallway. This building gave us several small offices and a small general meeting room.

After being roommates for a while, many of these groups chose to merge into one larger organization, The Sonoma County Peace Center. The Center would publish the *Peace Press*.

This coalition was a blended family and, like any other blended family, there were some difficulties adjusting to each others' ways of doing things. The Peace Network was made up primarily of people in their forties and fifties, many of whom were religiously oriented. Most had careers, house payments and families to take care of. These were professionals who had achieved success through the system and basically trusted the system. The SONOMore Atomics, Women Against Nuclear Destruction, Bohemian Grove Action Network and People for Peace in Central America folks were mostly younger, in their twenties and thirties, single or childless couples. We were renters, who wanted direct confrontation with authority. We felt that too much patience would kill us and we did not trust the system. Naturally, it took many meetings for these two groups to find ways to work together. For some, that was too hard and they quit. For others, the need for peace and disarmament was motivation enough to accept the differences in each other and make the changes necessary for things to work. It was clear that we'd need to develop actions with a variety of tactics so that those who wanted to risk arrest could, while those who didn't would have other ways to participate. A few people thought all direct actions were wrong as they were illegal. A few thought anything short of direct action was not revolutionary enough. Most of us could find common ground.

There were two core discussions. One was the need for justice to be part of our title. One group thought this made our title too cumbersome, and besides, they'd already printed the stationary. Others thought that there was no true peace without justice. It took over a year, but in the end, we chose peace and justice. Over time, I've seen other organizations across the nation make the same choice. My guess is that these people discussed the issue until they too realized that the road to peace is paved with justice.

The other core issue was what groups to let in. The older folks did not want to include the Communists. They thought this would discredit us. The younger ones insisted on it. We pointed out that it was the Communists who had been at the forefront of union recognition, of the forty hour work week, of the battle for overtime. They had made the sacrifices that the rest of us benefited from. The people who believed in the system were the hardest to convince. In the end, we decided to let the Communists in and then they never participated! More importantly, this issue molded us into being an inclusive, inviting organization that welcomed growth and change as the needs of the community evolved. This would turn out to be a most critical decision.

* * *

Within Santa Rosa lies the Community Baptist Church. It was led by Reverend James E. Coffee. He was a profound leader with a deep commitment to church, community and youth. The Church began holding annual birthday celebrations for Dr. Martin Luther King Jr. in 1981. These events feature singers, performers and speakers. There is an art show by elementary students and an oratory contest for secondary students, which was inspired by Cook Middle School Pincipal, Carole Ellis. This county-wide oratory contest produces two winners: one for 7th – 9th graders, the other for 10th – 12th graders. These young people speak before a panel of experts who judge their speeches. The winners are invited to address the audience at the annual birthday party. All the speakers are honored at the party. The winners receive scholarships of what I call magic money. What makes this money magic is that it consists of small contributions made during the year from people who don't know the recipients and contribute solely based on their faith in the youth to carry the torch forward. One of the early winners of this contest was Kenneth Duncan, who would go on to host the contest for decades to come.

Members of the Peace & Justice community participate in the birthday party and in preparing students for the celebration. In the years to come, the Peace Press would regularly feature speeches from the oratory contest. The celebration for Dr. King was part of Reverend Coffee's vision for his community.

Another part of his vision was to have a holiday to honor this man of peace. In 1970, California allowed schools to optionally observe Dr. King's birthday. Reverend Coffee wanted more. He was aware of the state-wide effort to make Dr. King's birthday an official holiday. He got in contact with the organizers and the Community Baptist Church led Sonoma County in our drive to make this a reality. Once again, members of the Peace & Justice community stepped forward to help with outreach, organizing and fund raisers. We helped, but it was the Community Baptist Church that drove this campaign for our county.

* * *

The greater bay area activist community is informed and inspired by KPFA radio station, 94.1 FM, out of Berkeley. It is the oldest of the five, listener sponsored, Pacifica Stations. By being listener sponsored, KPFA and the others are very independent voices for peaceful change. They are unbought and unbossed. Most of us listened to KPFA regularly.

On July 13, 1999, I was at my desk listening to Flashpoints, when all of a sudden the radio host, Dennis Bernstein, announced that Pacifica security guards were in the station, interrupting his show. They dragged him off the air, while I listened in stunned shock. There was silence, then elevator music. When the news came on, they announced what had just happened. The Pacifica Board put a gag order on the radio hosts. Immediately, they discussed it. Aileen Alfandary was fired. I couldn't believe it. Then they fired Larry Bensky and I knew they had gone too far. We needed to get our station back. I thought, what can I do? I wrote up a petition, addressed to the Pacifica Board, and hit the streets of Sebastopol. The owner of Incredible Records allowed me space in front of his store and I set up a card table with petitions for people to sign.

I was not alone. Pam put her button maker to work. Others created North Bay for KPFA, a large KPFA support group in Sonoma Coiunty, that organized carpools to Berkeley to join the crowds of folks, including Alice Walker, in the streets protesting the decisions the Pacifica Board of Directors were making. At one rally, Pacifica Board member, Pete Bransom, announced that the Board was planning on selling some of the stations, despite public pronouncements otherwise. The streets erupted with more protests, as the community rose up in defense of their voice. There had been trouble before, but nothing like this. Up in Santa Rosa, North Bay for KPFA organized held two benefit/teach-ins at New College. A number of KPFA programmers, including Dennis Bernstein, Walter Turner, Larry Bensky and others, spoke to a packed room. All over the greater bay area, people were mobilizing to save our station. Without it, we felt lost and disconnected.

KPFA is a contentious, scrappy station that attracts scrappy, contentious listeners. In the end, the Pacifica Board stepped down, Aileen and Larry were reinstated and not a single station was sold. Carol Spooner led a "listeners" lawsuit to remove the old Pacifica Board. New bylaws were written and elections held at all five Pacifica stations. Eventually, Carol Spooner and Attila Nagy of North Bay for KPFA, were elected to the KPFA Local Station Board.

* * *

As the new century began, The Peace & Justice Center moved to a permanent home on Sebastopol Ave., just around the corner from Julliard Park and across the freeway from Roseland, Santa Rosa's Latino community. With the move, we traded in a handful of small offices for one large space. Scheduling suddenly became important. We were in a new neighborhood, so when we held our first birthday party in Julliard Park the next year, we made sure to invite the neighbors. Our flyers for this celebration were bilingual, as was the celebration itself. Over the years, this annual party would grow and many elements of our greater community would be welcomed into the celebration.

Our awards ceremony was now large enough to be held at the Sebastopol Veterans' Hall. It included a dinner and speeches from the awards recipients'. Over time, we moved the ceremony to the Sebastopol Community Center and replaced the sit-down dinner with finger foods and a social hour prior to the awards ceremony. The Peace & Justice Center recognized activists categorically as Peacemaker of the Year, Community Organization of the Year, Courage of Commitment and Unsung Hero.

One community member, Sachiko, along with other members of the Japanese-American community, wanted to do something public in recognition of the tragedies of Hiroshima and Nagasaki. This idea had great appeal to the SONOMore Atomics folks and soon a coalition was born with an observation in mind. In 2005, the first annual Hiroshima Remembrance Day observation was held in Courthouse Square in Santa Rosa. This event featured speakers, some of whom had survived the internment camps and some of whom were atomic survivors. There was music by

Taiko Drummers, paper crane making and a closing incense ceremony.

This coalition wanted more than just a one day remembrance and decided to create Peace Poles. In September 2006, the city of Santa Rosa formally accepted one of these poles for Courthouse Square. These poles are five feet tall, white, six-sided and have the words "may peace prevail on Earth" written in twelve different languages on them. Soon, Sebastopol and other communities proudly displayed their poles, as the peace community grew more inclusive.

Another part of our community who organize for their rights is the Committee for Immigrant Rights. In 2008, this organization drafted a resolution to make Sonoma County a county of refuge, where the Sonoma County Sheriff would no longer collaborate with Immigration and Customs Enforcement (ICE).

On May first of that year, they organized the first Immigrant Rights May Day march. It drew an amazing 5,000 people! This was significantly more than the anti-war marches had drawn. An invisible part of our community was insisting on being seen and included. The Peace & Justice Center was among the first to join in support. Most of us missed the initial march, but by 2009, The Peace & Justice Center, The Healdsburg Peace Project, Petaluma Progressives, Code Pink and others were marching with our neighbors for immigrant rights. These marches started in Roseland, in the parking lot of a closed T G & Y, then proceed up the street to Julliard Park, where a celebration was held. Aztec dancers and drummers usually headed the parade. Workers, mothers with strollers, students, clergy, unions and many members of our community, marched in solidarity. Local merchants offered free water and apples and then, a block or two later, there'd be volunteers with one trash bag for the bottles and another for the apple cores. The community was clearly standing up for itself. The celebration in the park was a family-oriented fiesta, complete with music, food and friends. The first was great, the next better still and it continues to grow, year after year.

Not all the events in the Latino community were so celebratory. On October 22, 2013, at 3:00 p.m., a 13-year-old boy named Andy Lopez was crossing an empty lot used as a park by the local kids, when Sheriff's Deputy Erick Gelhaus pulled up and got out of his car. Andy had a toy gun in his hands that he was returning to a friend. Gelhaus ordered him to drop the gun. Before Andy could turn to comply, the deputy emptied his revolver, hitting the boy seven times, with the first shot killing him. The shots entered his back and side. He was never a threat to the officer.

This divided the community. The police protected their own, while the victim's family organized with others to fight for justice. The Justice Coalition for Andy Lopez (JCAL) was formed, consisting of the family, Andy's schoolmates, friends and members of the peace and justice community. The call from the community was for District Attorney Jill Ravitch to indict Officer Gelhaus. Students from Andy's school, Cook Junior High, organized a silent march from Cook Junior High to the County Government Buildings across town. Junior College students from the MeCHA Club provided security. The students were disciplined and silent as they marched. There were maybe six adults in the procession. When the marchers arrived outside of the County Buildings, they were greeted by platoons of armed law enforcement officers and marksmen on the roofs of the buildings. The marksmen were aiming rifles at the children. The marchers stayed disciplined. The organizers had planned on presenting their petitions calling for the indictment of Deputy Gelhaus to the DA in person but were stopped outside of the building by a wall of deputies. They spoke with the sheriff and he agreed to take their petitions inside to the DA. The protesters turned and quietly marched away.

In the months to come, there were petition drives, letters to the editor, speakers at events and on the radio, marches and many meetings with the County Supervisors. The Press Democrat supported the sheriffs. They continued to run the same photo of Andy wearing a knit cap, as they suggested that he flirted with gangs. They never showed pictures of him in his school band uniform with his horn. No, it was easier to reinforce racists' stereotypes. They blamed Andy's parents for letting him play with a borrowed toy gun when, in 2011 at the "Summer Day and Night Festival", the Santa Rosa Police Department's SWAT team had displayed real assault rifles before children and encouraged them to play with them. The lessons of injustice were not lost on the youth of Santa Rosa. The protests grew louder. Andy's classmates grew bolder. I saw young boys wearing balaclavas and carrying toy guns as they marched. This newly found courage barely contained their seething rage at the injustice of the situation.

One Saturday, Andy's family and lawyer went to the local mall. This is a place where working class people in Sonoma County shop. They went to the food court for lunch. They were approached by a mall security guard who told Mrs. Lopez that she'd have to remove her tee shirt as it was provocative. Her shirt had a picture of her deceased son on it. She began crying. The lawyer asked if there had been a complaint. There hadn't, but the guard stated that this was mall policy. Their lawyer then jumped up on a table and addressed the shoppers gathered there. He summarized the situation, then asked the crowd what they thought of all this. They voiced opposition to the guard. He called for backup. The lawyer argued with mall management while the Lopezes left in tears.

More marches followed. Around six months after the murder, students at Cook Jr. High staged a lunch time walkout and picket line. The principal locked them out of campus. They then marched to other campuses and attempted to gather other students for a county-wide walkout for justice. In some schools, they were locked out. At others, students joined them if they had to leap out of classroom windows to do so.

Following the election, the DA announced that she would not be prosecuting Officer Gelhaus. In 2014 you had a better chance of being shot by law enforcement in Sonoma County than you did by gangsters. That year, Andy Lopez was recognized as Peacemaker of the Year to a full house and a standing ovation at the annual Peace & Justice Awards Ceremony. Andy Lopez Presente!

The Peace & Justice Center has grown and changed over the years in very beautiful ways. What began as a largely professional class, Christian, white organization has blossomed into a multicultural, working and professional class, community organization that welcomes all who wish to live in a world centered around peace and justice.

VI

Sandinista

Two US puppet regimes were overthrown in 1979. In Iran, Shah II was disposed and in Nicaragua, the despised Somoza family was overthrown by a people's revolution led by the FSLN, the Sandinistas.

Meanwhile, in nearby El Salvador, the dictator Jose Napoleon Duarte's death squads had killed nearly 30% of the population. Here's how it worked. You'd wake up one morning and find a white hand painted on your front door with some Roman numerals under it. Those numerals represented the number of days you had left until the death squads would return to execute you. The message was clear. Run or die. Bodies with clear signs of torture were left by the roadside to terrorize the citizenry.

Ronald Reagan's team supported both the Somoza and Duarte dictatorships. As soon as the Sandinistas were in power, Reagan's regime began forming and arming an army made up of Somoza's National Guard, former death squad members and Argentinean neo-Nazis. They were called the Contras. Their goal was to use terrorism to overthrow the Sandinistas. Their strategy was to terrorize the civilian population so that the government would be forced to spend inordinate amounts of their budget on defense. Social programs would have to wait and this failure could then be used as a basis to ferment counter-revolution. It was a tried and true CIA strategy. The Contras were known to question people while aboard helicopters, then boot them out of the helicopters at several hundred feet up in the air. They used terror. They were terrorists.

The Duarte government in El Salvador was a terrorist government. Their death squads terrorized and murdered hundreds of thousands of people. Bodies were sawed in half. Decapitated heads and piles of children's hands were left by the sides of roads to frighten the civilians into submission. It didn't work. A civil war ensued, in which the government controlled the cities, while the rebels controlled the hills. Many fled the violence and headed north to the United States for sanctuary. The Reagan administration refused to recognize these Salvadorians as refugees from a civil war and sent them back to the very people who had tortured them.

The officers for these death squads were trained by the US at The School of the Americas in Fort Benning, Georgia. Here, students learn how to torture, how to extract information from prisoners and how to terrorize civilian populations. All of the training manuals are in Spanish. They are the enforcers of US corporate policy in Latin America. One of their graduates, Roberto d'Aubuisson, assassinated Archbishop Oscar Romero. Early in the 21st Century, The School of the Americas changed their name to The Western Institute for Security Cooperation, but we will always know it as The School of Assassins.

It was Eric and Cheryl who first brought these issues to the Radical Ions. They had been discussing them at their People for Peace in Central America (PPCA) meetings. PPCA was ready to take action, and they were inviting affinity groups to join them. We discussed the issues. Many of us welcomed this expansion of our resistance. Others questioned the effect it would have on our credibility as an anti-nuclear organization. Once we clearly understood US complicity with state sponsored atrocities, the decision became easy. We led with our hearts and embraced the issues of justice and peace for El Salvador and Nicaragua.

The Ions were changing. Jill was off for Taos, Bill and Linda for Israel and Elke for the Hog Farm in Tennessee. As the anti-intervention movement grew, we gained new members: Tanya, Pam, Judi and Eszter amongst them.

The Radical Ions decided to volunteer in three different ways. Most of us chose to educate our communities and raise money for organizations working to bring relief to the people in struggle in Central America. Some of us worked with the ACLU's Asylum Project and helped refugees reach safety in Canada through an underground railroad that stretched from El Salvador up the coast to Vancouver. Others went down to Nicaragua, to volunteer with the coffee harvest, Nicaragua's primary crop.

We weren't the only ones working for justice in Central America. There were Quakers, Catholics who'd embraced Liberation Theology, Friends of the Abraham Lincoln Brigade, socialists and others. One of them, a reporter for the Sonoma County Stump, Ben Linder, was murdered by the Contras while helping build a water system for a rural village.

The Friends of the Abraham Lincoln Brigade held their 50th Anniversary in Berkeley and used the occasion to raise funds for ambulances, on behalf of the people of Nicaragua. It was here, that Jennifer introduced me to Milton Wolff, the last field commander of the Lincoln's and a family friend of her's, stemming from her family's service with the Lincolns. Some roots run deep.

In 1981 Congress began investigating the nature of the Contras, or Freedom Fighters, as President Reagan liked to call them. Their investigations revealed numerous war crimes and in 1982, Congress passed the Boland Amendment to stop any further Congressional funding for the Contras.

The Reagan team decided to violate the law and began importing guns and other weapons to the Contras via John Hull's ranch in Costa Rica. Their planes had to leave the US without filing flight plans. Naturally, they'd have to return the same way. The Contras needed money, preferably untraceable money. What better source than drugs? The planes began returning to the United States with cocaine, specifically targeted for African-American urban areas.

The Ions were busy educating both ourselves and others. We developed our road show. We'd go to churches, union halls, senior centers, wherever we could. Some of us would be inside with a presentation that might feature slides or reports from people who'd seen the atrocities in Central America first hand. Sometimes, we'd have FSLN or FMLN speakers. While this was going on, others of us would be busy cooking spaghetti in the parking lot to feed people afterwards. Sometimes, we'd ask our audiences to contact Congress. Sometimes, we'd ask them for money. We always asked them to sign the Pledge of Resistance or the Pledge of Support.

The Pledge of Resistance committed the signer to engage in acts of civil disobedience, should the US invade Nicaragua. The Pledge of Support required the signer to engage in legal actions, should the invasion occur.

There were large marches in San Francisco, where thousands of people attended and signed the Pledges. People were organizing and fighting for the civil rights of the people of Nicaragua and El Salvador.

We met with our Congressman, Doug Bosco, and tried to educate him. Actually, we never met with him, but with his aides. We brought literature, photos and testimonies from people suffering in El Salvador. All we heard back was that the Congressman was working to keep us safe from the threat of communism. Anyone who'd been there could tell you that the issue wasn't communism, it was extreme poverty. We began sitting-in at his office and getting arrested for trespassing, trying to get him to stop supporting the war. Some of our outreach took the form of street theatre. We called these actions, the Guerrilla Girls. On tax day 1984, we did a Guerrilla Girls performance in front of the Federal Building. President Regan handed Death Squad leader Roberto d'Aubuisson a check from the American tax payer for his fine work in the assassination of Archbishop Romero. A Secret Service agent and a Contra soldier protected the ceremony, while Nancy beamed at her husband. Once the point was made, security escorted the party into the Federal Building with kazoos playing *Hail to the Chief.*

Paying for atrocities hurt many peace activists. Taxes for Peace offered opportunities for resistance by withholding tax payments. At one point, Eszter had to pay back taxes. A group of us, mostly Ions, joined her as she presented the IRS with her check, written on a coffin and consecrated with her own blood. There were photos of dead children in and on the coffin. Many of those bearing witness with her carried white crosses with the names of victims of US sponsored aggressions in Nicaragua and El Salvador written on them. The coffin stayed in the front office of the IRS for months before they called Eszter and had her remove it.

We continued to lobby our Congressman to stop the bombing. Judi wrote and performed her song *Where's Bosco?* when he wouldn't answer his constituents.

One day, while I was sitting at home, the phone rang. It was one of Bosco's aides. He'd called to ask me what it would take for us to like Doug. I was flabbergasted. I said I'd bake him a friging cake, if only he'd stop voting for dropping incendiary devices on women and children in El Salvador. The aide thanked me and I hung up. That was wild, I thought. I went next door to Monty's. As I entered his place, he shushed me and hung up the phone with an amazed look on his face.

"You won't believe the call I just got," he stated.

"Try me," I smiled.

Bosco kept voting for war, so we kept working for peace. To help promote war, Hollywood had released Top Gun. It was propaganda we needed to resist. This called for a Guerrilla Girls action. We went to the theatre. While people waited in line for the movie, a group of apparent "soldiers" marched in and began scrutinizing the people in line. Some of those in the line were Ions. The customers looked bemused or confused, not knowing what was going on. "General" Eric looked through his college yearbook as though he was matching photos. He had soldiers yank some of our people from the line. One ran away. She was shot. While this was happening, Robert stood atop a milk carton and addressed the people in the line. He informed them that scenes like the one they'd just witnessed were common in El Salvador. He told them how our taxes paid for this and that Congressman Bosco consistently voted in favor of these kinds of atrocities. Then we split.

When the Blue Angels did their recruiting performance in San Francisco as part of Fleet Week, we were in the bay with the Peace Navy, protesting them. Unfortunately, my political will and my stomach were not in agreement that day and while I hung over the side of the boat, feeding the fish, a sailor in a navy boat pointed a mounted machine gun at us and pretended to strafe us. The way I was feeling, I wish he had.

Nicaragua is a very poor country. When a supply boat showed up during a gun battle, the people defending the farmers created diversions while others unloaded the supply boat. The Contras, by contrast, never did without. They were well supplied with US armaments that flowed out through Port Chicago in Concord, California.

Port Chicago is the same port that weapons were shipped from during the Vietnam War. One strategy, was to stop the trains from reaching the ships by blockading the trains with our bodies. At one of these blockades, as Francisco Guerra was singing Love is Flowing like a River, a train approached a group of protesters waiting on the tracks. This group included members of Veterans for Peace. The train gained speed. The protesters held their ground. The train kept coming and Brian Wilson, an American veteran, was run over by the train. Miraculously, he lived. His head had been hit and he'd lost a leg at the knee. During the emergency surgery that followed, the other leg had to be amputated.

The movement exploded! The next day, thousands of people were at the tracks tearing them up with our very hands. We erected tombstones for Ben Liner, Archbishop Oscar Romero and the four murdered church women. Dozens of crosses for the thousands of unknown Salvadorians murdered by the Duarte regimes were erected. Soldiers stood behind rolls of concertina wire guarding the trains. They looked young and extremely nervous. I watched members of Veterans for Peace approached them with a body bag. "This is how you'll be coming home unless you think!" one of the vets announced, as they tossed the bag onto the concertina wire. The young soldiers looked nervous, the protesters were fearless and for a while, the trains were halted.

There was a rally in Santa Rosa's Courthouse Square which led to the dinner of my life. Towards the end of the rally Monty came to me and said that I was needed to provide a ride to San Francisco for Brian Wilson and Anna Cherny. We'd go along and hang out in the City until this very important dinner was over, then we'd bring her back to Sebastopol. I agreed. I knew of Brian, but I didn't know much about Anna. As we drove, I listened to Anna talk. She had been a secretary for the Party back at the first part of the century but was removed from that job due to her young age. She then started transcribing letters from Emma and John for People's World. That's right, Emma Goldman and John Reed. She was a suffragette and progressive activist. My respect for her grew, as I heard more of her history.

Following Brian's directions, we arrived somewhere in

the vicinity of Coit Tower. As we emerged from the car, I spotted our destination. It was a tower apartment across the street. A doorman in full livery stood at the entrance. We were wearing political tee shirts and jeans. Anna had on a mumu and hiking boots. No way are we getting in there, I thought. The doorman smiled and ushered us in. Monty and I joined the others, determined to ride this opportunity as far as we could. We road up the elevator and stepped out onto a carpeted hallway. I wondered where to go from there, then I heard voices coming from an open doorway.

"No, fuck that, send them guns," the deep, passionate, Brooklyn baritone retorted. "They need guns."

That's Milton Wolff of the Lincoln Brigade, I thought to myself, as I realized just how special this dinner was going to be.

We entered the apartment as a group. The party was held in a good-sized apartment that I gathered belonged to a movement lawyer. Our host was apparently too ill to join us, though he did come down briefly later in the evening. As uninvited guests, Monty and I were being very low key while absorbing everything around us. Monty and I are not easily intimidated and I must admit we were intimidated by the crowd at this party. As well as those mentioned, there was the Vice President of Nicaragua and the Nicaraguan Secretary of Education and Child Welfare. The Americans were speaking Spanish and the Nicaraguans were speaking English. Everyone was making an effort to reach out to each other. Meanwhile, Monty and I were physically up against a wall. I said no, and decided to mingle. I spotted this kind looking, little guy, stuck out my hand and introduced myself.

"Hi, I'm Rebel."

"My name's Lawrence," he replied.

"Oh, what do you do Lawrence?"

"I own a bookstore in North Beach."

Suddenly, I realized I was speaking with Lawrence Ferlinghetti, owner of City Lights Bookstore. Back against the wall for me for a bit.

The purpose of this dinner was to introduce people to one another on a social level so that political collaboration would be easier later on. The conversations were deep and more committed than I'd ever experienced before. The speakers carried their histories with them, and I recognized how important each of our actions are in the realization of who we become. The talk was polite, measured and focused on the practical needs for a revolution to survive. I listened much more than I spoke. It was exciting, for these people were birthing a new way of living, one I wanted for my own country.

In June of 1987, the call went out to shut down the Concord Naval Weapons Station. The first day drew media with a large front gate action. The Ions were doing a more dangerous, back country action the following day. Affinity groups were staggering actions to extend the length of the demonstration.

The next morning, as we were preparing for our back country action, we learned that the cops had broken a guy's arm at the front gate while the media recorded it. If the cops would do that at the front gate with the media present, what would they do in the back country? The thought was chilling. We exorcised our fears by opening up the doors to a car, cranking up the stereo and dancing our asses off to Aretha Live at the Fillmore. We bonded and rediscovered the strength of our love for one another in the dance. Now we were ready.

We arrived at a rear section of the base and approached the fence. There was an official sign hanging from it stating that the use of deadly force was authorized for trespassers. Some of us cut the fence. Others climbed over it. Once on the military's side of the fence, we formed up, unfurled our large red Sandinista flag and marched across the base. A soldier in a jeep pulled up and shouted halt. We ignored him and kept marching. Then two vehicles screeched to a halt.

"Somebody stop those assholes," I heard a voice command.

That's the boss, I thought, and sure enough, troops dispersed and we were wrestled to the ground. Even face down in the dirt, Eric managed to ask his arresting soldier how it felt to be a lackey for the war machine. I watched Robert yanked to his feet as a soldier pulled him up by his bound wrists. At his height, that was extremely painful. Two soldiers approached me. I was shoved to the ground. Each put a plastic cuff on a wrist, then left. I guess they each thought the other guy had finished the job. I found myself unbound, with plastic cuffs dangling from my wrists. Rather than risk a beating, I hollered out and they fixed that pretty quickly. We were put in a paddy wagon and driven all over the East Bay. Eventually, as it grew dark, we stopped at a 7/11. We were lined up and issued BART tickets.

I turned to Monty: "I just got issued a BART ticket for protesting the napalming of women and children. What does this mean?"

He said, "It means.....You put your left foot in/ you put your left foot out..."

And we did the Hokey Pokey and laughed, while confused cops scowled and protesters grinned.

Eric and I caught the BART back to the safe house and went into the tepee in the backyard to sleep for a bit. The following morning, we were back at the base. Unfortunately, another person in our larger group had naively assumed that the phones were safe and called his girlfriend to tell her what our plan was. We arrived at the fence, and when the first guy got to the top of it, a jeep skidded up and soldiers leapt out. We backed off and came up with an alternative plan.

We went to the headquarters of the Naval Command and blockaded the driveway. If we couldn't get in, they weren't going to get out. We sat there for a while, and then a tank pulled out onto the driveway from behind the building. It parked in front of us and scanned us with its cannon.

"Oh bullshit," Darlene stated.

She was right. After we jeered at it for a while, the tank went away. Soldiers came out and we were strong-armed off the base. Eventually, Darlene and Eric were arrested and released.

In October 1988, the Radical Ions decided to join the Steps to Freedom protest in San Francisco. We went down to the Presidio and blocked the street. This shut down Golden Gate Bridge. After a bit, we went to the base itself and dug a grave where we planted a coffin representing those killed in El Salvador and Nicaragua. Soldiers stood around us, silent and intimidating. Ions don't intimidate easily. We were arrested and taken to San Francisco jail.

This was real jail and not political jail. Barry tried to talk to some guys about the glorious, socialist revolution and they offered to beat him to a pulp. I spoke fast on his behalf and saved him from a beating. We were released after a few days.

The Ions met and did more work on El Salvador and Nicaragua. The Sandinistas were voted out of office in 1990 and the Americans quit attacking them. After a few years, American interests turned elsewhere and the Sandinistas were returned to power. In El Salvador, the FMLN became a legal political party and their candidates were elected to rule the country in 1992. Of the Ions, Judi moved up to Mendocino and when she returned for a meeting, she had some new ideas for us to consider.

photo by Evan Johnson

VII

Redwood Summer

Judi's new ideas fused her long time IWW-based unionism with her environmentalism. She presented these ideas to us at a Radical Ions meeting in 1990.

Pacific Lumber had been bought by a Texas banker named Charles Hurwitz. His company, Maxxam, had been culprits in the Texas Savings and Loan junk bond scandals. Hurwitz had kept out of jail by promising the government he would pay them the money, if they'd let him have a little time. He bought Pacific Lumber in 1986 with the intent of logging it all as swiftly as possible without concern for the workers or the environment.

Pacific Lumber was a company that had beaten the odds. Instead of the boom-to-bust attitude of most lumber companies, Pacific Lumber had practiced sustainable yield. If you talked with old time lumberjacks, they'd point out the trees they could cut, the ones they were saving for their kids and the ones they were saving for their grandkids. This practice supported lumber towns for four generations. The company was also debt free. This made it an underutilized resource in the eyes of Hurwitz and his Maxxam Corporation.

Judi was surrounded by this desecration at her home in the Mendocino woods. Felled trees were being taken out of the forests at ungodly rates. It seemed that every third vehicle on the freeway was an eighteen-wheeler with a load of old growth redwoods.

Rare redwood trees are economically valuable for one time use as goods. They provide much, much more as services. These giant trees are weather and soil stabilizers. They provide homes for countless species of plants and animals all throughout their canopy. Their deep roots bring minerals and nutrients to the topsoil. When they fall, they provide breeding grounds for the multitudes of life that follow. One of the forms of life that Maxxam's plans threatened was the Spotted Owl. This bird had been called an 'indicator species' by the Forestry Department. An indicator species is the first to feel changes within the environment. Like the canary in the coal mine, the Spotted Owl would be the first to fall. This made it a potent symbol in the war for the redwoods.

Due to her union background, Judi wisely realized that we needed to support the loggers in order to support the trees. This ran contrary to mainstream environmentalists who, as a crew, were white, college educated suburbites. Some of them saw no difference between the lumberjacks and Hurwitz. Judi realized that justice for the woods meant justice for the workers and that massive clear-cuts would result in massive job losses for the lumber towns in Mendocino and Humboldt Counties. In April of 1990, Louisiana Pacific Lumber closed their mill in Covelo, while posting record profits.

In March, Judi publicly denounced tree spiking. Tree spiking was a practice used by Earth First! that consisted of implanting a long nail inside a tree and then, when the logger cut the tree, the saw bucked and havoc followed. This had resulted in injuries to workers and clearly helped the timber companies' vilification of Earth First!. Judi denounced this practice the same month that she announced Redwood Summer.

Redwood Summer was an ambitious plan to fill the woods with eager, college students ready to do whatever it took to stop the clear-cutting of the ancient trees. Earth First! asked that participants adhere to a nonviolent code and activist trainings were offered with an emphasis on back woods actions in the forests. The model for Redwood Summer was Freedom Summer. Freedom Summer was when SNCC inspired college students in the north to travel to the south to register African-Americans to vote. It too, began with a massive statewide college recruitment campaign.

None of the organizers of Earth First! wanted chaos and people getting hurt. They wanted to save the trees and a way of life known in Northern California for generations. Judi met with loggers frequently to talk about their concerns and the changes that were occurring within the timber industry.

Lumberjacks had previously cut trees only after they'd grown to a minimum width. Hurwitz said, "We log to infinity", which meant an end to minimum width. He even brought in "feller-bunchers", which took down anything left standing following a clear-cut.

Like any other group, the lumberjacks were not of one mind. For some, Earth First! was a clear threat that needed to be stopped, no matter what. Other loggers saw that the trees were going much too quickly to last. The increase in the speed of tree extraction had created a boom in the timber industry. Like any other boom, it was designed for quick profits with no eye on tomorrow.

After the Ions meeting, Judi was off for Berkeley to meet with students. For Judi, this Ions meeting was an extension of that organizing. She knew her affinity group would be able to take significant action. Our first step in this campaign was to educate both ourselves and others as we rallied folks to defend the woods.

Judi, Darryl, Pam and Greg went up and down the state speaking at colleges and community centers. Their talks were inspiring and uplifting and they always included songs. Judi and Darryl sang in the tradition of the IWW, using familiar tunes with new, issue-oriented lyrics. Darryl played guitar and Judi her fiddle. These were joyous, empowering events and they were working. One could judge the success of the recruitment by the amount of anti-Earth First! propaganda that was flooding the mills.

The timber industry had been in decline prior to the Hurwitz' buy out. It wasn't hard to scare already frightened workers. This fear brought out the violent tendencies of either desperate people, or FBI agents. Death threats against Earth First! organizers were growing, as the timber companies tried to paint them as violent eco-terrorists. Earth First! used nonviolent tactics such as: picket lines, logging disruptions, banner hangings and tree sits in their defense of the trees. It was Julia Butterfly Hill's peaceful tree sit of over a year that had preserved the ancient redwood, Luna. Nonetheless, extreme efforts were made to paint Earth First! as violent revolutionaries. A picture of Judi playing her fiddle with a target drawn over her face made the rounds in the mill towns. People were playing for keeps.

Enter Irv. In 1988, Pam and Irv were roommates. They took a drive up to Mendocino County to visit Judi and Darryl. While there, Irv suggested that they take pictures of each other with guns in mock "terrorists" poses. Darryl and Judi joked about using the images on an album cover. Irv then pulled some guns from the trunk of his car, including an Uzi. Eighteen months later, photos of Judi cradling the Uzi began appearing in Northern California newspapers, alongside articles conflating resistance with violence. The photos were also sent to the FBI. Irv claimed that someone must have broken into his home and stole the pictures. Shortly thereafter, the FBI received a letter from "Argus" offering to spy on Earth First! and even offering to set up leadership for a pot bust. The details in this letter could only have been known of by four people: Judi, Darryl, Pam and Irv.

Judi and Darryl were provocative and unyielding during protests. Their songs, such as Where Are We Gonna Work When The Trees Are All Gone? and You Can't Clear-Cut Your Way To Heaven, were great organizing tools, and they pissed off some of the logger folks.

One time, Judi, Darryl and Pam were organizing for a rally in Fort Bragg, when a logging truck deliberately ran them off the road. The car was totaled, but the three of them, as well as Judi and Pam's four young children, survived, shaken, but okay. The intensity of intimidation was growing, so much so, that, following a beating, Greg left the state. Letters and death threats were discussed in the Anderson Valley Advertiser and other newspapers. When Judi brought up the issue of her death threats to the County Supervisors, Supervisor Marilyn Butcher replied, "Judi, you brought this on yourself." The government was refusing to protect environmentalists. The scene was ripe for more extreme violence.

I was at home when Kris-Anne called.

"They just blew up Judi!" she told me between sobs of disbelief.

I was not surprised.

That morning, May 24th, Darryl and Judi were leaving a house in Oakland when, as they crossed the railroad tracks, their car exploded. Instantly, the cops and the FBI were on the scene. Usually it takes a while for the cops to arrive, but this time they were diligent, almost as though they were expecting it to happen. Judi and Darryl lived, though Judi had a broken pelvis and internal damage and Darryl was in danger of losing an eye. They were both arrested for blowing themselves up. Clearly, the FBI's goal was to disrupt Redwood Summer. Being a top down organization, the FBI figured that if they took out leadership everything would crumble. Far from it. Others, mostly women like: Pam, Naomi, Anna Marie, Tanya and Karen took leadership roles and Redwood Summer kept moving ahead.

Most actions were back woods actions, where peaceful activist would sit in trees or chain themselves to equipment to stop the tree slaughter. These actions were extremely dangerous and called for the most delicate planning to succeed. Some people were beaten. One, David Gypsy Chain, was killed by a falling tree.

The first large action was in June, at the logging dock, in the town of Somoa. It was hairy! 700 people were at the rally, many others were blocking the road when the first logging truck pulled in. The Ions were amongst those who sat in the road to block the truck. The driver of the first truck leapt out of his truck screaming. How dare we deprive a working man of his ability to provide for his family! Just who did we think we were? Pam jumped up and faced the man, shouting back that earning a living was no excuse for clear-cutting the forests. We were challenged, and we did not back down. Forty-four activists were arrested that day.

In preparation for the blockade, Monty and I had made some cardboard overcoats that we painted to look like trees. We stapled fake money to them. We were wearing these overcoats while we were getting arrested. The cops twisted my arms so much that my head was upside down. It was in this posture that I was interviewed by CNN. Knowing brevity was the name of the game on TV, I shouted to the reporter, "No trees – No jobs", and was whisked away.

We were taken to the jail in Eureka. I was issued the standard, orange jumpsuit, only mine was several sizes too large for me. I was put in a group cell with many of the other men from the protest.

"I wish I had a cup of coffee," I remarked.

A cup of coffee was thrown at me from outside the cell. It drenched my head and arm. This wasn't the cup of coffee I had in mind. I wisely moved deeper into the room. My brother-in-law, Allen, was there. He'd been issued a jumpsuit much too small for him, one he couldn't even zip all the way up. We took one look at each other and quickly exchanged jumpsuits.

That first night was scary. All that day, we were taunted by unseen prisoners in other cells. They called out how they hoped Darryl was with us and how much they looked forward to beating us all up. We kept still. That night, the guards unlocked our door and opened it up to the hallway. I didn't know what to expect next. I looked around for a weapon. There was a pay phone attached to a wall. I tried yanking the phone off its line, but couldn't. I could only wait in silence. I didn't sleep much that night.

In the morning, we met and agreed that they were trying to mess with our minds. Okay, we can do better than they can. Using our imaginations and visualizing, we played a four person volleyball game. No net, no ball, just agreed upon visualizations.

At times supporters would wave to us from the street below. When the guards saw this, they chased them off. Once we noticed this, David S. and I would pretend to wave to people who weren't really there and then act like we were warning our supporters away. The guards would run downstairs to chase off, well, nobody. They fell for this more frequently than either of us expected. After a few days, we were taken to arraignment where all charges were dropped.

The next action was in July, at Fort Bragg. We had 2000 at our rally. Georgia Pacific held a counter-rally across the street from us. They brought out 1500 supporters and gave away free beer and hot dogs. The street between the rallies was no man's land. The more combative elements of both sides hung out at the roadway, taunting each other. One of the counter-demonstrators held a sign that read: "If you take my husband's job, he'll take it out on me". Several of our women went to talk with her.

Most of our focus was on the stage, where speakers and musicians like Pam, Darryl and Brian Wilson spoke and performed. Ben and Jerry's had a truck where an employee was giving away free ice cream cones to people.

The rally culminated with a march through downtown Fort Bragg. Counter-demonstrators ran by us, cursing us, as we sang and marched, until we came to the outskirts of Georgia Pacific's headquarters. The idea was to hold a brief rally, then occupy the headquarters. The Radical Ions went up to the edge of the timber company's headquarters. Cops were surrounding the place, roughly six feet apart from each other.

Meanwhile, at the rally stage, Darryl had just turned the microphone over to the community at large. Monty and I both considered this an irresponsible act. The first speakers were either hostile loggers speaking from fear or simpering environmentalists talking about love of nature. Then logger Duane Potter took the stage.

"You know me," he challenged the crowd. "Part of what these people are saying is true."

Everything stopped. Some people booed him, but this strong man stood his ground. People *did* know him and most respected him. Soon other speakers from both sides were making efforts to bridge the gap between us. The fear-based fault line the timber companies had worked so hard to build was dissolving and Judi's outreach to the loggers was paying off. We decided that a direct action on top of this would be counterproductive. After the rally, the Ions returned to Sonoma County. My last sight of the day was of the Ben and Jerry's guy sitting inside his truck, patiently bandaging his blistered fingers.

After Fort Bragg, the significant actions of Redwood Summer were back woods actions.

In 1989, prior to Redwood Summer, 150 people had protested the destruction of the forests. By August 1990, 3,000 more had joined them, with 150 getting arrested. Redwood Summer had succeeded and the struggle wasn't over yet.

The 60,000 acre Headwaters Forest was the last, unprotected stand of old growth redwoods on the earth. Maxxam wanted to log it and was planning to cut a wide swath, right through the middle of it, in order to destroy the ecological viability of the forest, so they could justify seizing the rest of it. The Environmental Protection and Information Center (EPIC) discovered this and stopped the cut with a lawsuit. The fight for the redwoods was now in the courts. Maxxam did not always respect court orders not to cut and back woods actions continued.

On New Year's Eve 1996, there was a huge mudslide that destroyed a third of the mountain town of Stafford. The houses were three to four feet deep with mud and debris. All of this was predictable, for lumberjacks had performed a clear-cut near the top of the mountain and then followed it with a logging road at the ridge. Then the winter rains came, and with them, the deadly mudslide.

A rally and a blockade followed. Over 1,000 activists were arrested and released. On our way home, Niki, Larry and I drove under a double rainbow.

Two carloads of Ions stopped at the River Road off ramp. There, we separated in different directions. That parting ended the final direct action by the Radical Ions affinity group. Most of us have continued to be politically active, however this was the last time we would all work together on a direct action campaign as the Radical Ions.

In 1996, Senator Diane Feinstein and Charles Hurwitz began making a deal for Headwaters. By 1998, the deal had evolved into a $440 million payment of taxpayers money to Maxxam for 7,500 acres of Headwaters Forest as a preserve. Feinstein and the liberals saw this as a victory for the environment. Some environmental activists saw this as little more than a tree museum. There is no report on what the Spotted Owl or the Marbled Murrelet thought.

In the years that followed, most of the mill towns shut down. In Bend, Oregon, the lumber mill that employed generations was replaced by the Old Mill Shopping Center, as Bend became a tourist town. Judi and Darryl sued the FBI over the bombing and eventually won. Sadly, Judi died of cancer before the settlement was reached. The money she was awarded saw her two girls through college.

My life was changing as well. I had become a teacher and for now I needed to find other ways to be politically active.

HHS Progressive Club

Educate, Empower, Act!

VIII

The Progressive Club

In 1995 I was hired to teach at Healdsburg High. I also agreed to be the advisor to the Environmental Club. The students of the Environmental Club adamantly did not want to recycle. Apparently student body leadership, ASB, had tried this the year before with disastrous results. I asked the students what they wanted to do with their club. Primarily, they wanted to learn what they could do to improve their own environmental practices. I got into the habit of bringing in articles from alternative press sources to give them suggestions. I'd been banking on the recycling being our primary activity. Now, I had to find something else for us to do.

At the next meeting I offered the students the chance to join the community in the annual Russian River Clean Up. That year, the first for Healdsburg High, five students from the MAYO Club (Mexican American Youth Organization) joined me in cleaning the river. The Environmental Club did not participate.

During the second year, we agreed to find sympathetic teachers willing to let us put recycling containers in their rooms. This was also the year a student brought up the issue of the annual wild horse slaughter in Nevada. Many members were outraged by this practice, though we took no action.

That second year all of the members of the Environmental Club were seniors and at the end of the year, they all graduated and left. I learned the lesson of the life span of club membership in high schools. The following year, the younger sister of one of the previous members came for one meeting and then I never saw her again. There was no Environmental Club in 1997/1998. I spoke with several of the more politically astute students I knew and they told me that while the environment was important, so were people. They were tired of just talking about the problems of the world, they wanted a club that would do something about them. Nothing could have made me happier.

In 1998, the Progressive Club was born with the objective of taking action on both environmental and social justice issues. The name came from an American social justice movement of nearly a hundred years earlier. Most of our members participated in the 1998 Russian River Clean Up. That was the year we also began fielding contestants for the annual Martin Luther King Oratory Contest. I also introduced the students to Amnesty International and their letter writing campaigns. Amnesty International writes letters of protest to the worst tyrants in the world, asking them to free nonviolent, prisoners of conscious and…it works. The public shaming and the sheer number of letters have moved many of these tyrants into improving conditions and even freeing some prisoners of conscious. This is not exciting work and encouraging students to write letters on top of their all ready busy school schedule was always challenging.

In 2000, the presence of military recruiters on campus had increased. It seemed like there was one on campus every week. Sometimes, they'd meet students at their classroom doors and publicly announce that they were taking their prospects out to lunch. It was sickening watching them dupe students with Big Macs and bling bling. I discussed this with the Progressives and they too wanted to stop the con job. I told them I'd find out exactly what we, as a school club, could do. I went to the Peace & Justice Center, where I learned that other school clubs had won the right to conduct counter-recruitment in the name of a balanced education. I thanked them and took what I had learned to the administration. They were reluctant, but recognized the law. It was funny, the vice-principal told me how proud he was of his service in the army and the principal told me how proud she was to have participated in a student strike against the war at her high school. The administration allowed us to table alongside the Army, Navy and the Marines whenever they tabled. I realized that this had to be civil or it wouldn't last and that the responsibility for this fell on me.

Our presence was met with a variety of reactions from students, staff and community. Some wanted me fired. Others blessed me for keeping their child from doing something stupid, like enlisting in the military. Veterans for Peace 71 and The Peace & Justice Center joined us on a couple of early counter-recruitment tabling. Their presence gave us some authority and they helped the students succeed. Every time we prepared to table, I grew nervous and wished I wasn't doing it. I hated the confrontation. Every time after we had confronted the war machine, I felt proud. Regardless of what people said, we, the Progressives, knew we were doing the right thing and that doing what was right was not always popular. It was only after the fact that we found out that the Progressive Club had been the first in the county to challenge the military so publicly. We became a model for other schools.

Then came the attack of 2001. While many called for war, we were a lonely voice calling for justice. We didn't agree that the killing of innocents could achieve justice by the killing of other innocents. The Progressive Club decided to join others protesting the war by marching in San Francisco. We announced these marches in the school bulletin as, "field trip on Saturday, with rides at the Flying Goat at 9:00 a.m.". The Flying Goat is a local coffee house and the

Healdsburg Peace Project organized the rides. When parents would contact me with concerns about the protests, I would tell them how the organizers, Act Now to Stop War to End Racism (A.N.S.W.E.R.), went to great lengths to make sure that the protests were safe. I usually invited them to join us. A few of them did and became peace activists themselves. The Healdsburg Peace Project helped immensely in both transporting and chaperoning the students, though chaperoning wasn't necessary, for the students always rose to the level of responsibility the situation called for and there were never any problems.

That year, we also held our first Earth Day Celebration. We were allowed to use part of the lunch quad. During lunch on Earth Day, we set up some student art, performed some music and provided speakers on steps students could take to preserve the environment.

By 2002, we had modified two garbage cans into public recycling barrels and placed them in the lunch quad. The level of commitment from these students was much stronger than from the students of the Environmental Club. These kids weren't afraid to get dirty to heal the planet. In 2002, our lunch quad cans and the handful of teachers who'd allow recycling in their rooms was the entire campus-wide recycling. We were proud of it and knew it was insufficient.

In 2003, two garbage companies were competing for a contract with the city of Healdsburg. The environmental consultants for each of these companies were friends of mine, including Pam. The competition was fierce and the company that finally won the contract donated thirty, twenty gallon, blue recycling barrels to the high school. Now the Progressives could organize door-to-door weekly recycling, which would not only promote recycling, but save the school money as well. The garbage company would charge for taking garbage and would remove the recycling for free. This sold it to the Superintendent. When I presented the idea at a staff meeting, most of teachers were on board. Now

I needed to find a way to sell the idea to the students. I remembered the previous students' reactions to recycling from just a few years earlier. I realized that I needed to find a way to do this so that they would want to recycle and that my enthusiasm alone would not be enough. Unbeknownst to myself, I had an ally on this; the students themselves. I had underestimated their personal commitments to the environment. At this time, the high school had a silent reading/study hall period. We used this time to study the practical applications of environmentalism. In other words, this was when we recycled.

The Russian River Clean Up was drawing roughly 10% of the student population now, with the Progressive Club and the MAYO Club both having a strong presence. For many years, we had enough volunteers to clean both Memorial Beach and Kennedy Lane. The Russian River Clean Up had become a tradition in a community that valued tradition.

The following Earth Day, we held a recycling contest where a math class made a giant rubric cube, a history class made a castle, and the winner, a science class, made a DNA strand from recycled cans. This class won an apple tree donated by Healdsburg Nursery which stands to this day outside of room 17.

We met once a week, during lunch, in my room. This is where we educated each other and planned our actions. The militancy of the students was growing. One day, as the meeting was beginning, I was told that I wanted a cup of coffee. I objected, but the students persisted. I left the room and walked around the campus for a while wondering what was up. I knocked and asked if I could come in. They said yes and we proceeded with our meeting. On the way home, I was listening to the radio when I heard about a pending student walkout against the war. At the next meeting, I told them two things. First, that schools make their required attendance quotas by lunch. Second, if you want to organize swiftly, one technique is to write your action plan on strips of paper and pass them out to the crowd at the last minute. Later that week, at the end of lunch, there was a student walkout against the war. I was immediately schlepped up into the principal's office and asked what I knew about it. I answered honestly, nothing. The students had given me plausible deniability. I never forgot this and it increased my respect for these brighter-than-average students.

At this time, the military's presence on campus was growing thicker. They were showing up two and three times a week, frequently unannounced, with their sales brochures and free gifts for the students. Many students were taken in by this and signed preenlistment forms, all just for some ego strokes from an adult and a Frisbee. The sight of it was nauseating. You see, students come to school trusting that the adults they'll encounter will tell them the truth and look out for their best interests. This makes them vulnerable to predators, like military recruiters. Our presence was more important now than ever before.

One time, a student asked the Marine recruiter if he thought that the Marine Band was a waste of money. The recruiter told him that those decisions were up to Congress and not him. The next week, we received a complaint about how rude we'd been. We hadn't been rude and the student was clearly upset by the accusation. We discussed what to do. I broke the news to them that it wasn't a level playing field and that the military enjoyed special privileges. They looked glum. I then told them that while the military was stronger, we were always smarter. The next time the recruiter came, that same student went over to him and told him that he'd taken the man's advice and contacted his members of Congress about discontinuing the Marine Band. He shook the recruiter's hand, smiling and beaming the whole time he spoke.

In 2005, we presented Cindy Sheehan as a guest speaker in a public forum on campus. This was our first presentation and it went very well. While a couple of community members made threats, many people, including both community members and students, listened and learned. Our hope was that this information would dampen enthusiasm for the war.

Over the next several years, we presented speakers such as: Peter Phillips of Project Censored, Jeff Paterson from Courage to Resist, Leuren Moret, a former military medic who specialized in radiation poisoning, Dahr Jamail, our leading unembedded journalist in Iraq, and media analyst Norman Solomon on campus. These presentations were held collaboratively with the Healdsburg Peace Project. We drew a consistent two hundred to three hundred people every time. Both students and community members attended them. We got hate mail too. As far as I knew, the hate mail always came to me. I tried to protect the students from the worst abuse. I used one of these hate letters to introduce Dahr.

Students were learning about the world beyond the confines of Healdsburg and college preparation. They were learning that they could be agents of their own destinies through hard work. It was their willingness to work that earned them the respect of our presenters.

Once I was followed home by a Marine recruiter. He threatened to beat my ass if I ever said anything bad about the Marines. I was shaken, but undaunted. The next day, I met with the Principal and she told me that the recruiter had made a complaint about my lack of hospitality. Expecting this, I handed her my complaint against him. She read it and grew quiet. She told me to go to class; that she'd take care of it. The Marines sent a different recruiter next time. I have been threatened by the Army, Navy and Marines. So what's up with the Air Force?

By 2006, we had a steady agenda: Russian River Clean Up in September, followed by the Petaluma Progressive Festival, often on the same weekend, the Martin Luther King Oratory Contest in December and January and Earth

Day in April. We did weekly recycling and monthly counter-recruitment.

That same year, we were the subject of a local documentary. It showed us at meetings, recycling and giving away plants and seeds at our annual Earth Day celebration on campus.

In 2007, we held our most controversial presentation to date with a forum discussing if George Bush should be impeached or not. The hate mail was heavy and I was prepared when I met with administration over it. We were going to be in the main theater and then, at the last minute, they moved us to the much smaller library. A sympathetic teacher offered us her adjacent classroom for the spillover crowd and we set that room up with a T.V. monitor. Nonetheless, the place was packed with four hundred and fifty people. It was a huge success.

In 2007, we also began working with the Climate Protection Campaign. We held teach-ins on campus where we reached around a third of the students on the then controversial subject of climate change.

In 2008, we expanded our efforts at reducing global warming by entering a climate challenge competition with Windsor High. This was done in association with the Climate Protection Campaign's Cool Schools Program. We joined in a coalition with the Peer Helpers Club and ASB. First, we conducted surveys of the distances driven by students and the number of passengers in the car for the ride to and from school. Our math pros used this data to calculate a baseline. Using this, we determined how much of a reduction was necessary to beat Windsor's rate. Taking into account the per capita difference in student populations, we needed to reduce our usage by 9% to beat Windsor. We promoted carpooling. We held an assembly to educate people. We asked community merchants for small gifts that we could give away to participants. We offered students cards that they could use to earn these valuable gifts. We then set up students at the entrances to campus during the half-hour before school and the fifteen minutes afterwards. These volunteers checked to see if people were walking, skating, riding bikes or carpooling. If they were, they got a stamp on their card. Once their card was completely filled, they could redeem it for one of the gifts from the community. The merchant would draw a line across the card when it had been used for a gift and return it to the student. We encouraged students to hang onto their cards for the big drawing on Earth Day. This helped tie school and community together on the issue of CO_2 reduction. One personal point of pride in this action was the pairing of a severally retarded student with an AP student at one of the entrances. They made an excellent team. We ran this contest for three weeks, as did Windsor. That year, at our on-campus Earth Day Celebration, we raffled off purses, gift certificates and even bicycles. To enter the raffle, you needed to have a completed card from any time during the three weeks that we ran the competition. In the middle of the celebration, our co-sponsor from Cool Schools arrived with the news. We had beat Windsor with a 12.5% reduction!

    In 2010, we conducted a very successful, campus-wide food drive with over 1400 items gathered from a student body of just under 900. We delivered this food to the nearly empty shelves of the local Food Pantry on the day before Thanksgiving. That spring, when we learned that one in six Americans had food insecurity, we used an abandoned part of the campus to begin an organic garden. This way we could supply our Food Pantry regularly with organic produce. In the process, we helped form a coalition between the School Garden Program and Farm to Pantry.

    That spring, we moved our Earth Day Festival off campus. Administration would never allow us an extended lunch period for our Earth Day Celebration as it wasn't educational time. It wasn't educational time because students had the option of participating or not. In 2010, this frustration peaked and we decided to move our Earth Day Festival off campus to the plaza downtown. This created a whole new set of learning experiences and fiscal challenges. We needed to raise $750 for the park. We increased our recycling and sold booth space for the festival. When we told the city parks department that raising $750 was hard for students, they informed us that by next year it was going to be $1400. We met the need. Through recycling and booth sales, the Progressive Club managed to raise the money required to hold free, educational shows in the Plaza.

While we were starting this mammoth undertaking, one of the Progressives went through a gender identity transformation. While this is not popular in the regular world, it is even less popular in high school. As second semester unfolded, we were down to two regular members and one part time member. Nonetheless, the regulars: Rachel, Aaron and I, plowed bravely ahead. It was always hard to recruit for a club designed for people who don't do clubs.

Suddenly one day, there were fifteen students present at our meeting, all excited about Earth Day and ready to work for the environment and world peace. I recognized some of them from the food drive. Rachel nearly cried when she came in the door. Nearly all of them were freshmen. That meant four years to develop an awesome crew. The Progressives were at a peak which would see us through to the end with willing, active, intelligent, creative, passionate students. That first public Earth Day rocked!

The Progressives of 2010 – 2014 were more interested in protecting the environment than in stopping the war, so our focus shifted accordingly. While they were still against the war, they wanted to discontinue counter-recruitment tabling, so we did.

During school-year 2012/2013, we held two educational forums, one each semester, in the school theatre. These forums each ran for forty-five minutes and we ran them all day long so that as many teachers as possible could bring their classes to them. We reached hundreds of students this way. One was on Fair Trade and the use of child slave labor in the harvesting of chocolate. The second was on Climate Change and actions students could take to combat it.

That year we took on a climate challenge and Earth Day at the same time. I felt assured that we had the personnel to do it. We managed to guide the student body into reducing the amount of $CO2$ they were putting in the air by one ton! Earth Day was again a huge success.

We produced our Earth Day Festivals in the Healdsburg Plaza for five years. We always maintained a balance of genders, ethnicities, peace and environmental focuses. Some of our Earth Day speakers have included: Project Censored, Miguel Molina from KPFA, Richard Heinberg, Norman Solomon, Alicia Sanchez, Our Green Footprint, the Committee for Immigrant Rights, the North Coast Coalition for Palestine, Mike McGuire, C. J. Holms and Russian River Keepers. Our dancers have included: HHS' Ballet Folklorico, Danze Azteca Xotel and the hip hop of Studio Gray/the Crew. Bands have included: Hoytus and One Heart, Happy Accident, HHS Jazz Hounds, Floral, Tricky Dick and the Hooligans, Secret Cat, De Colores, Peter Tracy, Gravity Hill and many more. We usually had around thirty booths from environmental and justice organizations who were there to do outreach to the crowd and network with other organizations. There were usually around three hundred people in attendance at any given time during the day.

Funding sources for Earth Day had grown with the need. SOAR Inflatables gathered all the trash that some of their customers tossed along the river while cannoning during the summer and gleaned the recycling from it. They then gave that recycling to us for further sorting and redeeming. This usually brought in $200 - $300. Councilman Mike McGuire donated $200 every year and we held Battles of the Bands to both raise money and select talent.

Once, ten minutes before school got out, Esther and

Aaron came to me and told me that we had no lights for our Battle of the Bands that night. I told them we could get mad, cry or find lights and that I knew what I wanted to do.

Within two hours, we had come up with a combination of Christmas lights, lights from the art teacher and a giant illuminated Christmas star that presented our shows better than if we'd used the school's lights. At that moment, we became the people who could do anything.

By 2013/2014, the club was down to eight students, six of whom were seniors. This was to be the final year of the Progressive Club. The Russian River Clean Up went well that year, with both the Progressive Club and the MAYO Club having a strong presence there. Our Martin Luther King Oratory Contest participant came in second, which is good. We held two Battles of the Bands. The one in November had a small turn out, while the one in February packed the theater to capacity. The musicians were impressive at both concerts.

The week before Earth Day it rained. It even hailed. The hail was so thick that highway 101 was closed for a while. On Earth Day, the sky was dry and the turnout was low. The day went very well with speakers from: the Russian River Watershed Cleanup Committee, Andy's Youth, Project Censored, the Peace & Justice Center, Fukushima Response, KBBF and CropMobsters. The Crew danced and we had music from a mixture of professional and student bands, as we always had done.

As the club drew to a close, we found that we had a significant amount of money left in our account. We decided to give our money to the Peace & Justice Center, the Middle East Children's Alliance and Clean Water Sonoma/Marin. The principal said there was education code against clubs giving money to organizations. I didn't believe him and I knew he had to approve all checks, regardless. School clubs give money to organizations all the time. No, it was our support of Palestine that killed it. As an alternative, we gave the money to the MAYO Club. They had always been present at the Russian River Clean Up and they were not afraid to work for what they wanted. We earned our money through sweat, work and some gifts. The MAYO Club also worked for what they wanted and we felt that they were the most deserving of our money.

The Progressive Club had been a success. It helped take intelligent, sensitive, active students into situations in which they have risen to peaks that they had never thought possible of themselves before. They have been exposed to worlds that the normal high school student is totally unaware of. They have gone on to work in central Africa, with girls' empowerment projects, the ACLU and fish hatcheries. Many have gone on to college where they have majored in environmental studies or law. They will be making their mark on America in the years to come. The baton has been passed.

IX

The War of Terror

Following 9/11 there was a loud call for war, as nationalism swept the country. The government manipulated our fears with a color coded terrorist alert system. People stole flags from their neighbors to show how patriotic they were. One man even wrapped his house in saran wrap to protect his family from chemical warfare. It was madness!

There were others who saw war coming and organized for peace. People demonstrated along the main streets of towns throughout America. I have seen peace vigils ranging from several hundred people to only two, up and down highway 101, from San Francisco to Willits. One group of citizens who protested the pending war was the Healdsburg Peace Project.

In 2002 the Healdsburg Peace Project held a rally in the town plaza opposing the imminent invasion of Iraq. Over a hundred people came. It was then, that the Healdsburg Peace Project began its weekly vigil along Main Street on the plaza. They were there rain or shine. Sometimes there were thirty of them, sometimes only one or two, but they were always there. At first they were met with boos, yells and people giving them the finger. A couple of cars even swerved at them. They persisted peacefully. As the war's lies became more apparent, the people giving them the finger began to be replaced by people giving them the peace sign and honking their horns in support. This took time and courage. It's not easy to nonviolently face verbal violence in the town in which you live, work and shop every day.

As well as organizing these weekly protests, the Healdsburg Peace Project brought speakers such as David Harris, Michael Parenti and Cindy Sheehan to Healdsburg. Later they would organize speaking events in collaboration with the Progressive Club. For two years, the Healdsburg Peace Project hosted a discussion show called What's Left on local access T.V. They started showing activist movies, primarily documentaries, for free, once a month at the nearby senior center. They also organized carpooling to San Francisco to join in A.N.S.W.E.R. protests.

A.N.S.W.E.R., Act Now to Stop War and End Racism, organized huge marches in San Francisco. Their goal was to bring out large numbers of people so that the government would follow the will of the people and not go to war. This belief in democracy was the dominate strategy for 2002 and the first part of 2003. To bring out lots of people, they invited a variety of progressive groups to join the marches. This unity illustrated how our diversity was our strength.

These marches and rallies were important events. People from all over the bay area came. There were Veterans for Peace, Code Pink, Women in Black, church groups and International Solidarity Activists. There were Korean activists wearing red tee shirts and First Nations People in traditional dress. A school bus of Veterans for Peace came down from Humboldt County, picking up vets along the way. The Peace & Justice Center organized rides from Sonoma County. There were marching bands that played both The International and Let's Impeach the President. The marches themselves consisted of lines of fifteen to twenty protesters walking abreast, chanting and singing for blocks and blocks and blocks and blocks. Many held banners, picket signs and other props. One group had a four foot by eight foot, wooden copy of the 911 Report that they carted around in a wheel barrel. It had several holes drilled in it to show the holes in the official report. There was a man in a business suit with a hardhat on his head. On top of this hardhat was a small oil derrick with a spring coiling out in front of his eyes. At the end of this spring was a dollar that he kept grasping for without ever quite reaching. Once I saw a man standing to the side with a hand painted sign that read "Republicans for Peace". He was in awe of what he was seeing and asked me what it was called.

"They call it democracy," I replied.

There were also tons of people in everyday clothes, sincerely doing what they could to stop their country from going to war. These marches frequently ran from the Embarcadero up Market Street to Civic Plaza, where a rally was held. Sometimes, a row of people would begin a low moan that would build up into a howling crescendo. Before that crescendo collapsed, the row in front of them would begin. The reverberations from these cries echoed off the concrete, glass and steel of the tall buildings of Market Street in an aural wave that bathed us in sound. At other times, the marches ran through the neighborhoods of the Mission District, where people came out of their homes to welcome us. Entering the Plaza, one saw long rows of booths from: the IWW, AIM, VFP, KPFA, Immigrant rights groups, Black Panthers, Move On, and others leading up to the stage. These booths offered information in the forms of books, flyers and discs. They often gave activists a chance to hook up with other activists and organize. Voter registration drives and initiative petitions were a common sight at these rallies. On stage, we heard speakers and entertainers such as: Dr. Edward Said, Joan Baez and Bonnie Raitt, Barbara Lee and Daniel Ellsberg. It was at these rallies that I first became aware of Michael Franti and Spearhead. The marches and rallies helped us realize that we were not alone. This realization led to greater acts of resistance, as activists left empowered, armed with information and ready to take on the war back home.

A.N.S.W.E.R. took security seriously. Nonetheless, there were a certain amount of agent provocateurs present at times.

As one march came to the rally site, we noticed a gathering of media around a small group of well-dressed people. These people held signs designed to offend. They had slogans such as, "I like the smell of burning Iraqis in the morning". A.N.S.W.E.R. peace keepers stood nearby, warning us that these instigators were trying to start trouble, right next to the press, so that it would make the news and obscure our message. We got it and kept marching. A man next to me slapped a bundle of papers from another man's hands in order to start a fight.

"What are you doin'?" I challenged.

"He's a Larouchite."

"You'll have to try harder than that, officer," I replied.

He turned bright red and faded into the crowd.

In Sonoma County, we first heard about these marches through KPFA, primarily Flashpoints. Further contact was made between A.N.S.W.E.R. and the Peace & Justice Center. These marches had unexpected benefits. At one we met Leuren Moret, Dahr Jamail and Jeff Paterson, which resulted in the three of them speaking at an event in Healdsburg that helped spread the word to those who couldn't make it to the marches in San Francisco. This wasn't the only time we brought the war home to Sonoma County.

It began with an e-mail from Barry, a challenge really. In it, he stated that collectively we all knew how to run a march and rally and that it was about time that we did so. He and Robin had acquired a parade permit and set a date to meet at the Peace & Justice Center to form the committee to organize it. Barry was right; we did know what to do. Rich was our lawyer, Robert helped with sound, I organized the peace keepers, Barry and Robin spoke on the radio and others lent their talents where they were needed. We invited other progressive organizations to join us. A poster and tee shirt were designed to announce our event, "A Day of Voice & Vision, March and Rally for Peace". The event was held on November 10, 2002.

We assembled on the lawn at Santa Rosa Junior College. It was amazing! As I walked towards the college, I saw people coming from every direction, dozens of them. I walked across the lawn and spotted Owen, Brian and Hannah from the Progressive Club. They had a white sheet spread across the lawn that they'd turned into a banner. It read Healdsburg High Progressive Club and the paint was still drying. They were proud to be there, as were most of the people I met that day. I got the impression that many of the people at this march had been privately against the upcoming war and felt that they were all alone. Now that they knew that they weren't, they were ecstatic.

We formed up to march. Our permit allowed us to march on the sidewalk, but with 3,000 people that was absurd. Barry spoke into a megaphone:

"A march ain't a march unless we take the street."

He led the way off the curb and was immediately confronted by a cop. Others stepped around Barry and the cop as they poured into the street. Traffic stopped. I spoke with the cops. We negotiated, and were allowed one lane to march in. We kept the marchers in that lane. We sang and chanted, as we waved our banners and signs to the startled traffic. Many drivers honked in support. After College Avenue, we took a second lane. The cops did nothing. When we were two blocks from Courthouse Square, we took the whole street. I could see a squadron of cops waiting for us up ahead at Courthouse Square.

At a given signal, we all let out cries and fell down dead in a die-in. The cops at Courthouse Square looked alarmed and started to move. We stood and began walking again. They relaxed. Then, half a block before the plaza, we died again. Owen asked me:

"Is this civil disobedience?"

"It is."

"Could we get arrested?"

"We could."

He nodded and trusted. As primary peace keeper, I was scanning the cops, wondering just how far we could push this. They began to come our way again. We let them start, then we stood and completed our march. The die-in gave those in the march a taste of the empowerment that comes from participating in direct action. This increase in militancy was the purpose of the die-in.

At the rally, we had booths from the Peace & Justice Center, Veterans for Peace 71, Women in Black and student groups with pamphlets, sign up lists and ways for people to organize with others. This was the largest march and rally Santa Rosa had seen since the war in Vietnam. It would remain so until the Immigrant Rights May Day marches of a few years later.

A.N.S.W.E.R. marches grew, as more people came out to stop the war. At the end of 2002, there were over 200,000 people in the streets of San Francisco. From the steps of City Hall one could see that, not only was the plaza full, but people had filled up the feeder streets for a couple of blocks in every direction. In January of 2003, we again brought out over 200,000 people to the streets of San Francisco. Then, on February 15, 2003, 13.5 million people from Taos to Tokyo, San Francisco to Beirut, New York to New Delhi marched for peace and those bastards went to war anyway!

On Sunday, May 30, 2003, we held our second march and rally in Santa Rosa. It was called "Bring the Troops Home Alive". This march began in Roseland and ended in Julliard Park, where the Peace & Justice Center was holding their annual birthday party.

We gathered in the parking lot of a closed T G & Y. The parking lot was large and many people had turned out. The mood was more militant than before. We used Tom's pick-up truck as a stage, with a small amplifier and a single microphone as our P.A. We needed to organize folks for the march. I agreed to get things started.

I climbed up rickety, metal stairs and looked out over the large crowd, wondering what to say. I started giving shout-outs to groups like Women in Black and Code Pink. They responded with cheers. This made it easy. I shouted-out other groups present like Cook Middle School and the Healdsburg Peace Project. The crowd was warming up. I turned the stage over to Barry.

We assembled and headed out of the parking lot. Aztec dancers and drummers led the march. Most of the organizers wanted to be near the front, so I opted to stay in the middle, where the majority of the students were. We filled Sebastopol Road with chanting, drumming and singing as we marched through the streets. At Mendocino Avenue, we turned south towards Court House Square.

Once we hit Mendocino Avenue, the police tried to confine our march to the sidewalk. This wouldn't do. There were thousands of us, and we were empowered to act. People waited for the police to pass, then took a lane, only to be pushed back as we marched. They kept trying. It became a tug of war between democracy and order.

"Whose streets?" Barry called into the megaphone.

"Our streets." The marchers shouted back, as they continued to demand their right to march in the streets. I was proud to hear that the Progressive Club had been at the spearhead of those challenging the police.

Our march ended in Julliard Park, where we brought an additional 3,000 people to the Peace & Justice Center's annual birthday celebration. On stage, a local mariachi band was playing as we entered. Speakers representing: the community, Congresswoman Wolsey, the Peace & Justice Center, Veterans for Peace and the Committee for Immigrant Rights spoke. There were booths from: Taxes for Peace, the Petaluma Progressives, Women in Black, MeCHA, A.N.S.W.E.R. and the Peace & Justice Center. These booths provided information and opportunities for people to organize with others in search of peace.

The Peace & Justice Center was deeply involved with

peace activism at this time. Elizabeth Stinson, the director of the Peace and Justice Center, helped develop two anti-war programs. One, H.O.P.E. (high school and college outreach peace education), conducted counter-recruitment on campuses throughout Sonoma County. The other, a collaboration with the Military Law Task Force, helped service personnel separate from the military. By 2006, this program had helped over five hundred active duty members separate from military service. I knew the outreach was working when I heard a soldier say that he'd read the phone number of the Peace & Justice Center on a bathroom wall in a Greyhound Station. Now that's outreach!

Sonoma County can be proud of its radical anti-war activism. As the threat of war turned into war, peace activists shifted from protest to resistance. One member of the Healdsburg Peace Project had acted as a human shield in Baghdad to try to stop the invasion. She was there when the sky exploded.

Back home, the Healdsburg Peace Project had begun marching in the annual Future Farmers of America Parade. This is Healdsburg's annual big event and everybody in town is either in the parade or watching it. It represents the community and the Peace Project thought it was high time that peace was represented in the parade. Robert obtained the permit, while other members created colorful costumes and props. Then we marched.

In 2006, I was invited to drum in the marching band. That evolved into a rock n' roll cover band called the Flaming Wheel Barrels (of love) and lasted until 2009, when we transformed into the more radical, originals band, Happy Accident.

By 2007, the Healdsburg Peace Project's entry in the FFA Parade included a flatbed truck and electric music. I was sitting at home, waiting to load the drums onto the truck, when John drove up on an orange tractor, towing the flatbed. The tractor was powered by biodiesel. The flatbed had been decorated with paper flowers, Buddhist prayer flags and tissue paper. Paper streamers ran along the tractor from the grill up both sides to the driver's seat. There was a throne for our Goddess, Marylyn. She was in her 80's and needed to ride for her legs and walk for her heart. She did both, with a giant, jeweled peace sign glued to her forehead. The Peace Project's parade crew included: the Healdsburg Peace Project, the Progressive Club, The Healdsburg Day Labor Center and Sonoma County Conservation Action. It was something else to ride down a street on the back of a truck, playing electric music outside, while Canadian geese flew overhead.

We turned the corner onto Center Street. That's when the parade became intense. We had a boy of around ten who was watching the parade from the plaza. He had a peace sign painted on his face. A man said, "Peace. Piece of shit." and decked the kid, dead on. Many adults rose in condemnation of this act, regardless of the politics.

I heard about this afterward, for I was on the float, playing drums to La Bamba, when an unknown woman leapt onto our float and started talking in the microphone about how President Bush was protecting us with the war. Aaron, the singer/bassist who'd just lost his microphone, looked stunned. I chucked a drum stick at her. She stepped off the float, just before we came up to the judging booth.

"What do you think of this shirt," challenged a judge in an American flag, rodeo shirt.

"I think it stands for the 80% of the country who want our boys home now!" Bob shot back and chaos ensued.

"Keep moving," the announcer commanded.

"Not without a song." Bob replied loudly.

So we played *War*, while Doug drove that tractor slower than I thought a tractor could possibly go. We dog-eyed the judges the whole way, as members of the Peace Project chastised the announcer for his lack of respect.

A week or so later, a member of the parade committee dropped in on our band rehearsal. He wanted to know what we wanted. We told him we wanted the same respect as Bill the barber or Betty the beautician.

Protests continued, both in San Francisco and at home, as the war rolled on. At A.N.S.W.E.R. rallies Cindy Sheehan, Medea Benjamin and Jeff Paterson spoke of war resistance and support for those troops actively resisting the war. In Washington, Representative Dennis Kucinich gave Congress thirty-five reasons to impeach George Bush. In Healdsburg, the Peace Project, in collaboration with the Progressive Club, held a forum on impeaching Bush. War resistance was growing, and we in Sonoma County wanted to do more.

Robin called for a meeting at the Peace & Justice Center so we could develop a stronger presence at the next A.N.S.W.E.R. march. We decided to hold a funeral march, complete with coffins and victims. We went to U.P.S. and bought six cardboard coffins. We painted them black. While some people were doing this, others of us made lanyards featuring photos of victims of the war. We wore these lanyards during the march. The idea was to mourn this one person, so that death wasn't an abstract number, but was the tragic loss of that individual. We used pictures of both American and Iraqi victims. We covered parts of the coffins with additional photos of victims of the war. These were gruesome photos, mostly of civilians. Finally, the coffins were covered with American, Iraqi and Palestinian flags. We dressed in black for the funeral march. Other mourners joined us, as we proceeded up Market Street from the Embarcadero to Civic Center Plaza. At the rally, we "buried" our individuals by removing our lanyards and dropping them inside the coffins. I felt the loss of my individual personally when I surrendered mine and it furthered my commitment to end the war.

Marches continued. Letters, meetings with Congress, nothing seemed to stop the war. It was time to up the ante. It was time for Occupy.

Occupy Wall Street began in September 2011 as an outgrowth of the Arab Spring. It spoke of classism, a subject rarely, if ever, discussed in the land of the free. Both the

Arab Spring and Occupy began for the same reason. In both cases, the governments were unresponsive to the needs of the people. The US government bailed out banks, but not homeowners. They had money for war, while veterans' benefits were cut. Student fees skyrocketed, as corporations received tax breaks for sending jobs overseas. The middle class was collapsing. Occupy framed this perfectly with the brilliantly inclusive slogan "We are the 99%".

Occupy's tactic was to occupy public spaces, starting in Zuccotti Park, in New York. This soon became Liberty Plaza. Occupiers would gather in a large circle and hold public meetings, called General Assemblies, to decide their course of action. People shared freely. Food Not Bombs came to the forefront with Occupy. Food Not Bombs had been around for a while. They were based on a simple concept: government needs to take care of the poor and not waste money on wars. To this end, Food Not Bombs would set up tables in parks and other public places where they would distribute food and anti-war information. Had they been giving out food and Jesus, they would have been left alone, but by challenging the state, they were constantly harassed about permits and other bureaucratic hurdles. They were one of the groups present at Occupy. There were a lot of familiar faces there. There were also many new faces as well, faces of those suddenly disenfranchised, the recently unemployed and the newly homeless. They were there with nowhere else to go.

Initially, the press ignored them. Then, in early October, protesters dressed as zombies descended on Wall Street. Now they were noticed and soon their ideas were being discussed everywhere. Before Occupy, the Federal government was focused on the national debt. Once Occupy came along, the focus shifted to issues of class.

Occupy spread from New York to Chicago and Oakland and to smaller towns like: Taos, Tucson, Laramie and Fargo. It sprung up in cities throughout Sonoma County and when Occupiers needed support, the infrastructure of the

Peace & Justice Center was there to support them. This movement was a combination of experienced activist and energetic youth. Many of the more astute political activists I knew, such as Robert and Linus, were swift at recognizing Occupy's potential. Linus and I even got our union local, HATA, to endorse Occupy. We all realized that the overt tactic, camping in public spaces, was unsustainable. Once Occupy was recognized by the media, there was a conference of mayors. Shortly thereafter, the police began cracking down on occupations. They seemed to target college-aged, white women, though others, most notably veteran Scott Olson, were also seriously assaulted by the police. Occupy moved from the parks to embrace issues of class, such as student debt (Occupy our Debt), foreclosures (Occupy our Homes), public water access (Occupy Sacramento) and urban agriculture (Occupy the Farm). Class warfare was on and resistance was strong.

Occupy Oakland worked with the Longshoremen and other unions to bring about a shutdown of the Port of Oakland. This was the first such shut down since 1946. 15,000 people were there. Robert and Heidi, experienced campaigners, reported that when they arrived, they walked through the crowd for hours and never made it to the front of the rally. There were that many people there. It was impressive and demonstrated the power of the 99%. There were actions throughout Sonoma County too, including: occupations, leafleting, marching, picket lines and community organizing.

On May Day, 2013, we met in Courthouse Square as part of the national Move Your Money Campaign. Food Not Bombs fed us as we planned our day. The goal was to get as many people as possible to move their money from the worst banks, the ones most responsible for home foreclosures, to more ethical financial institutes, like credit unions. Around here, the villainous banks came down to: Chase, Citibank, Wells Fargo and Bank of America.

We went to the branches of those banks located around

Courthouse Square and started handing out flyers about their crimes to the people we met. Our flyers included a list of honorable banks and credit unions people could turn to as alternatives. I stationed myself outside of Bank of America. Bank of America made my job easier by shuttering their doors for the day. Those closed doors angered their customers and simplified the act of directing former customers to more honorable institutes. The other targeted banks around Courthouse Square also locked their doors. Without intending to, we'd shut down the most sinister banks in our immediate area. Wonderful!

Following five hours of leafleting, I was all tuckered out. I joined others in a nap on the police station lawn. We were napping there because Santa Rosa had just passed a law against sleeping in public and we wanted to challenge this classist law where we couldn't be missed. First they make us poor, then they criminalize us for it. There was no way we were going to tolerate that. Jasmin read us modern fairytales as we took our naps.

Following my nap, I joined others, as we rose to unite with the Immigrant Rights May Day march forming up a few miles away. Before we left, we were offered seed bombs. These were seeds, gently wrapped in thin layers of clay and about the size of a walnut. As we walked along Santa Rosa Creek, we threw those seed bombs towards the creek bed and waited for the seeds we'd planted to grow.

X

NCCP

We were born out of the atrocity of the attack on the Mavi Marmara. The Mavi Marmara was one of the ships in a flotilla who, in September of 2010, had set sail across the Mediterranean to challenge Israel's illegal, naval blockade of Gaza. In an act of piracy, Israeli Special Forces boarded these ships and murdered nine unarmed activists. Israel claimed that their attack had been an act of self-defense. Only Israel can spin an act of piracy as an act of self-defense. Mary sent out an e-mail in which she poured out her pain at the situation in Gaza and asked others who were as wounded as she was to show up at the Peace & Justice Center to organize resistance. I was expecting five or six people, all of whom I'd know, to show up. Instead I was pleasantly surprised to see the room packed with over fifty people!

We sat in a large circle as each of us explained why we were there and what we hoped to achieve at this meeting. There were a variety of opinions as well as different degrees of understanding about the situation. Some people wanted to learn more before taking any action while others suggested immediate material support for the Palestinians. There were people who thought of this as a war between two opposing nations and didn't realize that it was a colonist/indigenous struggle with all the power dynamics that implies. There were people whose main concern was with Israel. They wanted to start a dialogue group. In order to address everyone's needs we set up several groups all under the umbrella organization of the North Coast Coalition for Palestine Support. I was attracted to the Boycott, Divest, and Sanctions (BDS) action group.

BDS was started in Palestine in 2005 and is supported by the overwhelming majority of Palestinians. It calls for a boycott of all products and services profiting from the occupation until, minimally, Israel allows overseas Palestinians the right to return home in accordance with UN Resolution 194, Palestinians living in Israel enjoy full civil rights, and Israel withdraws from the illegally occupied territories in the West Bank and elsewhere in accordance with UN Resolution 242. I thought this was the route to take as it followed the will of the Palestinians.

Within a month all the groups except the BDS group had dissolved. We became NCCPS.

The first year was tough. Building an organization with different perspectives on how to structure it was a challenge. Some people wanted Therese to be our leader. Those of us who had come up through the anti-nuclear movement were appalled at the concept of leaders. Some people wanted majority rule while others preferred consensus. There were people who thought that the government would respond if only they knew how bad it was while others thought that the government was complicit in the oppression. This later group favored direct actions that could result in arrests. The idea of being arrested horrified some of the other people. Clearly a lot of discussion was in order. It took over a year to find out what we as a group wanted. We ended up making decisions by consensus unless it got tough and then we resorted to majority rule. During this first year I nearly quit many times. Every time I thought of quitting I thought of doctors in Gaza who know what to do to save lives but, due to Israel's illegal blockade, lacked the supplies needed to save their patients' lives. Mostly, I saw an image of a small boy with a rock in his hand facing down a tank commanded by an adult wearing Kevlar and holding a machine gun. I had no problem knowing which side I was on and my petty ego bruises shrunk in importance when weighed against the pain of a child. I stayed with the group. It was a struggle and I was not the only one struggling with it. Some folks quit. Others kept trying and over time the love we developed for one another made missing a meeting a drag. Through struggle we became closer to one another.

One of the most difficult issues we had to resolve was over our cumbersome name. We went around and around on this for over a year and in the end all we did is take out the word support so that we became the North Coast Coalition for Palestine (NCCP).

Our group was made up of: Christians, Jews, non-religious folks, atheists, Muslims, and pagans. We were Euro-American and Palestinian-American. Early on we took a stand denouncing racism and anti-Semitism. We wanted to make it clear that we were not an anti-Jewish group.

As we grew we took on projects. This combination of developing as a group while creating events helped weld us into a unit. It was a struggle and our love made the struggle fruitful.

Our first goal was to educate the public and counter Israel's dominant narrative. We also needed to make some money to fund our organization. To do both we decided to hold public events. It was time for Palestine to step from the shadows.

Our first public presentation was a performance of the one woman show *My Name is Rachel Corrie* along with the Middle Eastern folk dance/singing group Aswat. The event was held on February 13, 2011. We rented a hall, made flyers, wrote press releases and planned our show. I was in charge of security and had my eyes open for trouble as I worked the door. I was worried, yet nothing bad happened. Instead scores of people showed up who were overjoyed to be there. As I watched people coming into the theatre it seemed to me that many of them had thought they were alone in their concern for Palestine and now that they found out they weren't they were empowered. We also accidentally tapped into two audiences at this show. Many Euro-Americans were there for the play while many Arab-Americans were there for the dance/music performance. We began to cultivate a regular audience made up of local Euro-Americans and Arab-Americans.

Many of us went to Palestine/Israel during these years. We worked directly with the Campaign to End the Occupation, the International Solidarity Movement, Global Exchange, Jewish Voices for Peace, and others. This put us in contact with people from all over the world who were working with this international movement.

Our group got tighter. We presented educational films and speakers including the films *Budrus* and *Five Broken Cameras* as well as speakers like Anne Wright, and Laila Hadad. We learned of this one guy, Kenny who, all by himself, was doing the same kind of outreach down in Petaluma. We quickly swopped him up, much to his delight. He went on to help initiate Sonomans for Justice and Peace in Palestine. We also presented the poet Remi Kanazi. We went to many festivals with tabling material to educate folks and raise funds. Therese and Lois became our public faces as they spoke at events and provided commentary for both the newspaper and the radio.

In June 2011 the Break the Blockade Flotilla challenged Israel's illegal blockade when the Audacity of Hope set sail for Palestine. Israel said they'd stop the ship anyway they could. NCCP called for peaceful protest downtown should Israel respond with violence. The ship was in Greece preparing for the final leg of her trip. Tensions were building until Greece succumbed to the pressure and held the Audacity of Hope in port. We did press interviews and protests calling for their right to sail and pointing out the illegality of Israel's blockade of ports.

It was time to start enacting boycotts. We needed to know which products to boycott in order to plan our BDS actions. To learn this we went to "Shop Israel". We began with Soda Stream.

Soda Stream sells a machine that puts bubbles in your drinks. It was made on occupied Palestinian land. Soda Stream was carried locally at Bed Bath and Beyond, so that became our first target. Lois and I went into the store and met with the manager to let him know that there would be pickets in front of his store today protesting Soda Stream. We assured him we were not protesting his store, just the product they were carrying.

We had people outside handing out flyers to customers explaining how Soda Stream used stolen lands to make its product. There were perhaps eight of us there. The mall cop came up and told us to split. I informed him of the Pruneyard Decision, a court ruling that recognizes the public nature of malls and shopping centers and allows for first amendment activities as long as the protesters allow entrance to and egress from the store. The cop split and came back with a Santa Rosa cop. We continued to picket and hand out flyers while explaining the law to this cop. A third cop showed up and spoke with us before they got it and allowed us our Constitutional rights of protest. We were successful. Deppen filmed it and posted it on YouTube. We congratulated ourselves while realizing the limits of ad-hoc actions. For all that effort and success we had made a very small dent in the liberation of Palestine. We needed to work with others in order to enact serious change. We hooked up with Jewish Voices for Peace, End the Occupation, and Global Exchange. We decided to join the international campaign to stop Veolia.

Veolia is a French, multi-national corporation that runs,

but does not own, the Sonoma County buses. They also run buses in the illegally occupied West Bank. These buses run on segregated roads that serve only Jewish customers. This made Veolia an ideal BDS target. The County Board of Supervisors hires the bus company that runs our buses. Our goal became to convince our Supervisors to not renew Veolia's transit contract. The contract review was in 2014 with the full contract up for renegotiating in 2016. Initially we decided that we would try to gain the support of the County Human Rights Commission prior to approaching the Supervisors. We thought that the Commission's recommendation would help us reach our goal. We knew we had a lot to learn. We got a lot of help from Anna Baltzer from End the Occupation, Sydney Levy from Jewish Voices for Peace, and Dalit Baum of Global Exchange.

In preparation we developed our web site, nccpal.org which included a tool kit for activists. We studied other propositions and based ours on what we learned. We met, talked, studied, and prepared our case. We divided our forces and got to work. Eszter, Irene and I wrote the proposal, citing the Universal Declaration of Human Rights, the Rights of Indigenous Peoples, and the Commission's Mission Statement. Nick and Therese prepared their testimonies while Lois wrote a press release. Others did research that added to our documents. We planned. Knowing we needed to be on the agenda for the commission to take action, we scheduled our presentation for July 24, 2012.

Prior to the hearing we presented the eleven members of the Human Rights Commission with a packet that included both our resolution and pertinent historical references. We gave them supplemental materials in the forms of books, pamphlets, and DVDs. We knew that Veolia would also be lobbying the commission prior to the hearing.

During the late afternoon of the day of the meeting we gathered over a meal and made our final preparations. The plan was that Nick, Therese, and Anna would present our case followed by Veolia's presentation. A one minute community input session would follow. It was during this time that many of us would speak. We knew other people from the community might also want to speak on our behalf so we put talking points on slips of paper to pass out to our supporters. We vetted people before we gave them the slips as we did not want to arm our adversaries. We had to be security conscious as there were Zionists there bent on our failure and destruction. We also passed out green, self-adhesive "Investigate Veolia" stickers for supporters to wear.

When we arrived the meeting hall was packed. The anteroom was packed. There were people in the foyer and all the way down the steps to the parking lot.

Chairperson Judy Rice began the meeting by denouncing our proposal and stating that it fell outside the mandate of human rights. She said this was why two commissioners weren't in attendance. Then the "fair" hearing began.

First Nick and Therese presented fact based statements illustrating clear violations of human rights that were being supported by Veolia's infrastructure. They were followed by Anna Baltzer from End the Occupation.

Veolia spoke next. Their side included two Veolia lawyers, Chief Ethics Officer Alan Moldawer, and the Vice Counsel of Israel from San Francisco. They and their supporters denounced us as anti-Semitic terrorists. They even said our proposal was illegal; that it violated the Export Administration Act. Well, this act forbade boycotting friendly countries and, last I checked, Veolia is a company and not a country, beside the damn law sunsetted back in the early 80's.

The one minute presentations followed. Mostly it was one minute trade-offs from different citizens group. NCCP and the Jewish Community Relations Council both offered speakers. They called us anti-Semites, Kapos, and terrorists but provided few if any facts. We presented heartfelt testimonies from local folks including Christians, Jews, Muslims, and one Holocaust survivor. Dalit countered Veolia's claim that they no longer owned the Tovlan landfill. This landfill processes Israeli garbage on Palestinian land. Volunteers from Who Profits had called Tovlan on Sunday and the Veolia representative seemed surprised anyone would think they didn't own it. Clearly these guys were lying. No wonder they earned the name Veoliar.

The meeting went on for over five hours. When the vote to consider recommending our proposal to the Supervisors came down it was a four to four tie, forcing Chair Rice to cast the deciding vote. Our recommendation failed and we gained a ton of support and press. The Commission grew confused and friendships shattered while we grew stronger. Bolstered by our success we decided to approach the Supervisors directly. But first we needed to strengthen our game.

The Sonoma County Board of Supervisors had taken a stand against apartheid in South Africa so there was a precedent for our proposal. We met with some of the people who'd organized that action and learned. We studied and focused our actions. We realized that we needed to do three things: 1) build a coalition of groups influential to the Supervisors, 2) frame our issue in as positive a light as possible, and 3) do most of the work ourselves so that our ask was very small. Our plan emerged. Goal: justice and peace in Palestine/Israel. Strategy: nonviolence via BDS. First target: County divestment of bus lines from Veolia. Pivot Point: the Board of Supervisors. Tactics: coalition building, education, outreach, films, speakers, tabling at festivals, speaking, letters to the editor and blogs, petitions, supporting our allies in achieving their goals, lobbying each supervisor individually and focusing on what moves that particular person. We were ten to twelve people. Our new coalition grew a name and a web site. Sonoma Allies For a Fair Ride (SAFFR). It means to travel in Arabic. Our site was SAFFR.info

Building allies took real work. One night I went with my Navy vet friend, Linus to a meeting of Veterans for Peace 71. We sat in a circle on folding chairs in a cold Veteran's hall. There was one woman. Each person explained why they were there. Some were damaged. Some were helping others. It was a group struggle to undo the damage given them by the wars. Then the introductions came to me. I never was in any branch of the military. I introduced myself as a lifelong peace activist and that was honored. I valued that respect for I know that it's groups like Veterans for Peace who are the real backbone of our movement. I went out into the parking lot and looked at the stars while they discussed the issue. After a short time I was called in and they announced that they would join SAFFR.

One by one we made alliances with various church groups, Fair Trade, Project Censored, Racial Justice Allies, several peace and justice groups and many Middle Eastern groups. Organizing with the national groups was weird. Initially we'd get thumbs up from them and then a few days later there'd be hems and haws and backpedaling after they'd talked with their parent organization and were forced to withdraw their support. It seems someone larger then NCCP was influencing them.

On September 15th we spoke at the Progressive Festival in Petaluma. We passed out post cards for people to sign which stated that they wanted a more ethical company than Veolia to run our county buses. Each card was addressed to the person's specific county supervisor. We had five neat little stacks tied in red, green, and black ribbons. We knew the postage would be deadly so we decided to drop them off in person at the Supervisors' office the next day. This was not meant as a threat. We'd called the Supervisors in advance and told them we were coming, as neighbors, doing what was best for our community. We invited them to join us. We dropped off the cards and everything went as planned.

A few days later I got an e-mail from the Supervisors' secretary with an attachment. The attachment was a letter Veolia's Chief Ethics Officer, Alan Moldawer, had sent to the Supervisors on September 13th, two days before the festival. In this letter he condemned our speaking at the festival before the fact, linked us to the League of Arab States, misrepresented the bus drivers' contract, and denounced Omar Barghouti, founder of BDS, as promoting euthanasia of Israel! I know gold when I see it. I thanked the secretary for sending me the letter. I contacted the others and soon lawyer letters followed. The story was picked up by Electronic Intifada, National Lawyers Guild, Daily Censored and other media, and then, on September 25th, we heard through reliable sources that Veolia had sold their segregated bus lines in the West Bank! It's nice to think that, along with Boston, St. Louis, Yolo County, and others we had a part in that strike for justice.

We held a victory party, for victories are few and far between and need to be celebrated. We decided to push for changing the bus company in 2014, though 2016 seemed more likely. While the Board could optionally review the contract in 2014, they were required to renegotiate it in 2016.

In December we caroled at the local mall with a variation of O Little Town of Bethlehem, a cardboard wall, and a handout about the twenty-six foot wall that surrounds the city today. The holy family would probably not have the proper IDs to enter Bethlehem today. The action was very successful. We watched parents explaining the issue to their children and we picked up a new member from Novato during the event. Surprisingly we weren't thrown out by mall security. I was prepared with copies of the Pruneyard Decision should they arrive. I figured I could talk long enough for us to finish the song and split. We never needed to do this and we performed the song several times. Omar filmed it and put it up on YouTube.

We held more events including a very positive one where we simply stood on the street with I love (heart) Palestine posters. People supported this positive approach and it affected the protesters in energy renewing ways.

That year there was a BART strike and Veolia came to

the assistance of BART management. New alliances were formed between the BART drivers, Palestinian activists, and communities injured by Veolia. There was a BART rally at Oscar Grant Plaza in Oakland where I spoke for nearly three minutes denouncing Veolia. Coalitions built.

In January we joined unions, internationalist, environmentalist, and other justice activists for an all-day forum called "Stop Veolia" at the Mission Cultural Center. It was filmed and put on YouTube. We brought Rabbi Lynn Gottlieb to Santa Rosa to speak about the injustice of the occupation and then, on March 23rd, we presented Omar Barghouti to a full house.

In June we testified to the Supervisors at the review hearing. They voted unanimously to postpone taking action until they have to in 2016. It was what we expected and we'll be back with our allies. Until then we have more organizing and educating to do.

In July I left Sonoma County. NCCP has been very busy with Israel's most recent invasion of Gaza. New people have joined up. It's unfortunate that it takes tragedies like the butchery in Gaza to bring people out but it does. The struggle continues and it continues without me for this is where my voice fades and others pick up the tune. It's a simple song. Anyone can sing it. Find your voice and join in the chorus. If you do you'll find your verses. Lift your voice and let freedom ring.

Coda

So what did all that mean? Was it just fun and games or were there results? Let's see.

Not a single commercial nuclear power plant has been built in the US since Diablo Canyon went on line. More people are aware of the dangers of nuclear power than ever before. On the other hand, the threat of total nuclear annihilation is still with us. The people of Nicaragua and El Salvador have freed themselves of despotic rule and created their own destinies under the leadership of the Sandinistas and the FMLN respectively. The Peace & Justice Center is an established presence in Sonoma County. The wars drag on, highly mechanized and far from the media's eye, while activists continue to work for peace throughout the county. Headwaters is a preserve and not cut lumber. Occupy has morphed into several, target specific, localized, direct action groups. Israel has become more of an isolated pariah with every atrocity they commit on the Palestinians. We've had a lot of success and there's still a lot of work left to do.

Hundreds of thousands, perhaps millions of people have participated in these campaigns. Most of them have been changed by their experiences. For many people, political activism is like LSD, in that it opens doors that, once opened, can never be shut again. Activist live longer. Political activism changes people for the better. Let's use the Radical Ions as a case study.

Most of us were in our twenties, single and done with school. As the years passed, we developed families and careers. Our careers reflected our politics. Darlene became a civil engineer. This is a field where there is never a line to the women's room. Her strong, feminist skills enabled her success. Pam's feminist strengths and environmentalism led her to become the manager of a local recycling plant before being appointed to the County Planning Agency. Tanya formed the Purple Berets, an organization that defends the rights of women in domestic abuse cases and, at age sixty, became a lawyer. Robin's skills as a fund raiser benefitted many progressive organizations. Larry worked with wood, while Elke became an organic farmer. Monty evolved into a counselor, helping unemployed lumberjacks in Oregon. Barry, once he adjusted to having Parkinson's disease, lent his enormous strength to the Disability Rights Movement. Robert became one of the county's first solar electricians and continues in the field to this day. Eszter and I both taught at risk students for years. I don't know what happened to everyone, but I can assure you that none of us became corporate lawyers or hedge fund investors. We all sought right livelihoods.

I retired from teaching and moved up into the mountains in 2014. This is the most beautiful place I've ever lived. Everywhere I turn there are mountains, creeks and soaring condors. Wind tears through the tall trees along the ridge tops. Katydids and crickets serenade the night. Deer, turkeys and California Crows are everywhere. When Israel attacked Gaza, I was sitting under some poplars and pines, looking out over a lake as ducks flew overhead and turtles played in the mud below, and I wept. I wept because people were suffering and I could do nothing about it. People are born for many reasons. I was born to fight. I can't enjoy paradise while children lie bleeding in the streets; I'm too much of a Bodhisattva for that. I'm returning to the fight. Let me clear my throat, find my C and raise my voice in song. Why don't you join me? Together, in harmony, we can make this world a better place. I promise you that your life will be enriched by it. Yours in peace and justice – Rebel

Acknowledgements

First off, I want to thank John for the thumb drive, Niki for the ride off the mountain and into town twice a week and the Willits and Santa Rosa Public Libraries for the use of their computers and printers. Support your local library. I also want to thank Omar for all his help in layout and turning my manuscript into this book.

Next, I want to thank the individuals who lived these adventures with me for their amendments to my memory. These include: Barry, Robert, Mary, Larry, Eszter, Terra, Attila, Pam, Therese, Lois and Wayne. In addition, I want to thank Mary, Peter and Alicia for their kind words. I also want to thank Holly Near, whose music permeated the movement.

I didn't rely on memory alone. My research tools included: the Diablo Canyon Blockade/Encampment Handbook, Livermore Weapons Lab Blockade/Demonstration Handbook, Alan Snitow's report on Livermore, as heard on KPFA, Norman Solomon's book *Made Love, Got War,* Carl Sagan's *Nuclear Winter, The Untold History of the United States* by Oliver Stone and Peter Kuznik and many back issues of the *Sonoma County Peace Press.* I also referenced Sharon Wood and Veronica Selver's POV video *KPFA on the Air,* Noam Chomsky's *Turning the Tide, Timber Wars* by Judi Bari, *BDS* by Omar Barghouti and the video *Who Bombed Judi Bari?.*

I want to thank the Movement and everyone in it for working so hard, for so long, to make the world a better place. Thanks for a future.

(continued from back cover)
battlefields. From Diablo Canyon & Redwood Summer to the Bohemian Grove & Occupy, Rebel Fagin brings an insider's view on the importance of individual commitment and activist's solidarity for successful resistance to the injustices of the powerful. It is a book well written from a life well lived.
  – Peter Phillips, Media Freedom Foundation/Project Censored

As a social justice activist for over 40 years, I feel it is wonderful when someone remembers the past activists/activities. Reading Rebel's book made me cry, and made me realize that so many of us can feel proud to have been a part of so many social justice struggles mentioned in his book.

Reading it gave me hope and confirmed my belief that when we see a need, an injustice, a simple wrong, there are always people who when gathered together, will make it right. In unity there is strength. Rebel is one of those people who is always there.

I am so happy that Rebel chronicles these struggles enabling us all to remember and keep on moving forward by recording the past struggles so we can learn from them to inform future struggles.
  – Alicia Sanchez, Union/community activist, board president of KBBF radio, the first bi-lingual public radio station in the USA

www.ingramcontent.com/pod-product-compliance
Lightning Source LLC
Chambersburg PA
CBHW032139040426
42449CB00005B/319